from CONCEPTION *to* BIRTH

OUR MOST IMPORTANT JOURNEY

Dr Tony Lipson is a Pediatrician, Fetal Developmentalist (Dysmorphologist) and Geneticist at the Children's Hospital in Sydney, Australia. His practice and internationally respected research is concerned with babies who have birth defects, genetic disorders and incomplete patterns of development. He is therefore ideally placed to consider normal patterns of development.

Dr Lipson is married to Anne, a social work therapist, and has three sons.

DR TONY LIPSON

from CONCEPTION *to* BIRTH

OUR MOST IMPORTANT JOURNEY

MILLENNIUM
BOOKS

First published in 1994 by
Millennium Books
an imprint of E.J. Dwyer (Australia) Pty Ltd
3/32–72 Alice Street
Newtown NSW 2042
Australia
Phone: (02) 550-2355
Fax: (02) 519-3218

National Library of Australia
Cataloguing-in-Publication data

Lipson, Tony.
  From conception to birth.

  Bibliography.
  Includes index.
  ISBN 1 86429 006 4.

  1. Embryology. Human – Popular works. 2. Fetus – Growth –
  Popular works. 3. Pregnancy – Popular works. I. Title.

612.64

Edited by Marg Bowman
Copy-edited by Dawn Hope
Cover design by Megan Smith
Text design by Megan Smith
Typeset in 11/13½ Garamond by Post Typesetters, Brisbane
Printed in Malaysia by SRM Production Services Sdn Bhd

10 9 8 7 6 5 4 3 2 1

98 97 96 95 94

CONTENTS

ACKNOWLEDGMENTS

Many thanks to Dr John Buttsworth and Emily Donald for encouraging me to write this book in the first place; to Professor Bill Webster, Professor Marshall Edwards, Dr David Walsh, Dr Trish Woodman, Mimi Lee, Dr Debbie Wass, Dr Avril Earnshaw, Derek Molloy and John Said, Dr Christine Rogers and the Solar family—Jack, Misha, Leslie and Marina—for their advice and inspiration along the way; to my many friends who have related their own babies' prenatal experiences; to John Buttsworth and Christine Rogers for kindly reading the early drafts and providing much input and to Miss Michelle Giaquinto for her patient secretarial work.

Margaret Gee provided some astute criticism and suggestions. My editor Margaret Bowman approached the task of changing cherished phrases and hackneyed comments with great sensitivity. As an embryo author, I couldn't see the tautologies, jumps in logic, grammatical errors, and medical terminology, which Margaret deftly corrected without bruising my ego.

My thanks also to the many "pioneers" in research and to those who have used this knowledge of the prenatal environment in practical ways. I have tried to acknowledge their contribution by name, in the text. Truly I am "standing on the shoulders of giants" who have preceded this work and also my interest in the subject.

1

The Beginning of Life

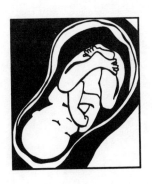

Man and woman are in turn embryo, fetus, infant, child, adolescent and adult. We change continuously, not only in form and substance but in the activities we perform and the things we experience. Today, people seem most concerned about the development we undergo as infants and children, and then as adolescents, middle-aged adults and as old people. These stages of our lives are of great concern and interest to us all, but over the last 10 or 20 years, research has enabled us to learn more about our life *before* birth.

Birth, although a significant physical and emotional event for our parents, particularly our mothers, is a comparatively insignificant event in our own development. We are nine months old at birth, but our most significant growth and development have already occurred by this time.

The womb is the child's first world. The changes that occur before birth and their importance in our later development easily eclipse all that comes after birth. Those first nine months are crucial in determining and influencing our physical and psychological life. Despite what philosophers, teachers, scientists and others have thought in the past, when in the womb we are not in a stuporous state, nor are we, as the great French 18th century philosopher Rousseau indicated, a "tadpole with a mind like a cleanly washed slate". The New Zealand obstetrician Dr A. W. Liley, one of the first doctors to try to diagnose and treat diseases in fetal life, describes the fetus and newborn not as a poorly functioning adult but as a superbly functioning baby, totally adapted to its environment and developmental stage.

Although our conscious memories may not retain our prebirth experiences, these experiences nonetheless have a crucial role in our postnatal development. For good reason did the ancient Chinese and Japanese have prenatal clinics; not, of course, for the purpose of dispensing iron tablets, vitamins and taking blood pressure, but rather to ensure the tranquillity of the mother, in the belief that this would benefit the unborn child.

Although their ideas about pregnancy were often governed by superstition, primitive cultures also show remarkable insights into life before birth. They had taboos warning women away from stressful events and harmful practices. All such cultures held the view that a woman is able to influence the looks, health and character of her unborn child and advised a variety of practices to prevent a difficult birth or the birth of a child who had an abnormality. Many of the reasonings and practices seem ridiculous in the light of modern science, but this should not take away from the fact that for ages people have realized that prenatal influences are important for the development of the baby, that there is a "life before birth".

Today this knowledge has elicited a greater respect for the processes of embryo and fetal development and the role they play in influencing our later life. When we look at a baby, we consider, quite reasonably, his or her development to be immature and rudimentary according to our adult standards. Yet experiential learning does not start at the moment of birth, but well before. A proper regard for this life before birth will help us understand ourselves, our children and the process of life itself. It will also help to prevent many of the problems of pregnancy and birth which occur during the newborn and baby period. As well, it will enhance the baby's learning and personality development, increase family cooperation and reduce the incidence of risk factors related to the raising of children.

We should not assume that the baby is completely dependent on its intra-uterine haven for its development. The drama, pain and ecstasy of birth should not detract from the importance of prenatal influences. The light of the labor ward does not signal the start of external influences on development: it is just that they now occur in a way that is more direct and obvious. The road we all travel is influenced by our environment and interaction with those close to us; what could be closer than the baby in the womb and its mother? The mother provides the home, the warmth, the food for the little life she carries; living in the same "house", the baby will be influenced by what is happening in that house: the mother's diet, movements, feelings, sounds, smells, the fears, the joys, the love, the arguments, and the nurturing. Knowledge of the facts of fetal development can really contribute to our understanding of how parents and society can help this new life, not just after, but before birth.

In The Beginning

For each of us life begins at an unfelt, unhonored instant when a minute, wriggling sperm plunges headlong into a mature egg. The quiet egg, destined to die and rot unless it fuses with the sperm, reacts with vigorous activity and a spurt of energy. At this moment, known as fertilization, not only does a separate entity come into being, but also its unique individuality. This entity has been endowed with a mysterious but important quality that is called viability, or the ability to live, able to survive the trials and adversities of life before birth, as well as life after birth in nine months hence.

In this book, we will look at the successes and failures of those first nine months, when the new life is being changed from a nondescript, microscopic blob of living matter into the squalling baby that enters the world at birth. But first we shall take a closer look at the very beginning of that new life.

The mystery that surrounds sperm, ovum and fertilization only became evident when the microscope was invented, enabling scientists to observe these structures in animals. Prior to the use of this scientific instrument, people puzzled about the origin of life, coming up with many fantastic theories.

One theory which was accepted for many hundreds, if not thousands, of years was that man provides the form and woman the substance, the woman being purely a receptacle and a nutritive force for the form, and the soul and spirit being contributed by the man. In the words of Aristotle, the famous Greek philosopher, "... if we think about ourselves as a statue, man is the sculptor and woman is the marble". This remarkable theory persisted and historically still influences our attitudes, despite being, in the light of modern science, nonsense. Goethe, the famous German philosopher of the 18th century, put it in a different way in his verse: "From my father I received my form, my dignified and earnest state—From my mother my ebullient nature, and tendency to fabulate (!)" The guilt that a woman may feel when her baby is born with a birth defect has its origins in these ancient theories.

When the early microscopes revealed the sperm, they were at first thought to be microbes or germs. In fact, the term "spermatozoa" means "semen animals". Scientists ran riot with descriptions of a fully formed human, the Homunculus, or "miniature man" within the sperm. Miniature animals were also seen in animal sperm, the ears of the donkey even being described in donkey sperm! As the microscope was not strong enough to define exact form at high magnification, imagination was able to take over.

It took a long time before the realization came that both man and woman contribute to the origin of life. With the theories prevalent during medieval times, it must have been pretty puzzling for our forebears to observe basic genetic inheritance. Certainly, however, it did not appear to stop farmers all through the ages from husbanding their animals to produce successful and functional breeding by expertly using the genetic material of both female and male. There must have been a lot of unwritten knowledge and truth handed down.

William Harvey, a great English scientist who first described the circulation of the blood through the heart in the 17th century, also made an equally important observation based on investigations and studies carried out on dissected deer belonging to Charles I at Richmond, near London. He concluded that we do all indeed come from an egg, this conclusion being a monumental step forward in scientific understanding of life before birth. His work *De Generationale Animale* (The Generation of Animals) is lesser known than his famous treatise on the circulation of blood through the heart called *De Mortu Cordis*, and he was only heeded because of his great stature as a scientist of the time. He also described the stepwise formation of the organs, finally laying to rest the fantasy of the preformed or "miniature man". However, it took until the modern era to determine where that egg came from and what the individual contributions of man and woman were.

Once it was recognized by Dr Rudolf Virchow in Germany in the 19th century that the cell is the fundamental unit of the organism, it became possible at last to comprehend the process of fertilization, as a fusing of two germ cells.

The numerical discrepancy between egg and sperm production is massive. A male uses up about 300 million sperm in a single ejaculation. Ova or eggs are used sparingly, and in the female a single egg matures at monthly intervals throughout the reproductive period, which means that only about 500 ova or eggs reach maturity and leave the ovary in the lifetime of a woman. Amazingly, in the human female the development of ova occurs before birth. This means that by the seventh month of pregnancy all female cells or eggs have already commenced the first stage of their development into mature ovum in the fetal ovary. They then remain quiescent, only one of the 400,000 ovum or eggs in the ovaries coming to maturity at each ovulation.

The ovum is the largest cell in the body, with the possible exception of some nerve cells. Even so, it measures only one 128th of an inch or 0.2 millimeters in diameter. All the people alive in the world today developed from ovum which would fit into a cake pan! The sperm is one of the smallest cells and the difference in volume between sperm and ovum is 80,000 times, the sperm being about 2 thousandths of an inch long. Laid side by side in a long line, the sperm that created all the people in the world would extend a little over one inch only! The sperm contributes only its nucleus or gene material to the ovum or egg.

The ovum also contains other structures which up until recently were thought to be carried along for the ride. These structures, which contribute to the utilization of oxygen, are called the mitochondria; they contain DNA that will contribute to genetic inheritance, in addition to supporting the chemistry of the ovum itself. If defective, they can result in disease in the life being formed.

This important and curious form of inheritance called mitochondrial inheritance means that the functions mediated by these genes, and diseases

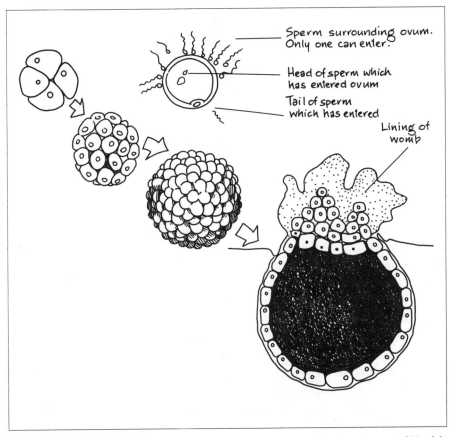

Sperm surrounding ovum. Only one can enter.

Head of sperm which has entered ovum

Tail of sperm which has entered

Lining of womb

EARLY DEVELOPMENT. *From* Pregnancy and Birth, *New South Wales Department of Health. Used with permission.*

resulting from their malformation, can *only* be transmitted by the mother, but can be passed on to both boys and girls. These diseases often result in defective muscle function.

Sperm, in contrast to the ovum, do not develop before birth, but are continuously formed in the testicles after puberty, the original germ cells multiplying millions of times. It takes two months to manufacture a fully mature sperm, the sperm being produced at a rate of 1000 per second. The journey of the ovum is only one inch before fertilization, but the journey of the sperm is long and hazardous. Before the sperm can accomplish its sole purpose in life, fusion with an ovum or egg, it travels over a distance of more than 16 inches through the coiled sex ducts of the male before being ejaculated. Then by lashing their thread-like tails, sperm are able to swim at approximately 6 inches an hour, though they are helped by rhythmic muscular contractions of the uterus and fallopian tubes.

Energy for this swim comes from absorbing the normal vaginal secretion of lactate, a type of sugar. Without this friendly environment, the sperm would not have the energy for its marathon swim.

OVULATION

Ovulation is the expulsion of the egg or ovum from the ovary. It usually occurs at mid cycle, about two weeks after the start of the menstrual period. Fertilization by the sperm can then occur over the next 48 hours. The sperm can remain viable for up to 48 hours so that intercourse before ovulation can cause fertilization. The rise in temperature and the change in vaginal mucus (factors used in the Billings method of contraception) are used to signal this most important event. Sometimes there is a sudden pain in the side of the lower abdomen to signal the extrusion of the egg from the ovary. Cycle variation is common, however, and ovulation can occur throughout the cycle.

Most women and obstetricians measure the length of a pregnancy from the last menstrual period. The true timing occurs on the average two weeks later, which may lead to confusion. The developmental timing of organ development, dealt with later, will use true gestational timing. Clearly some of the variation in the actual timing of the pregnancy can be due to cycle and ovulation differences.

THE GENES AT WORK

Fertilization takes about 24 hours, starting with the penetration of one, and only one, sperm into the egg or ovum. Once the sperm passes through to the inside of the ovum, a chemical reaction occurs and a surrounding protective layer forms around the ovum, making it impermeable to other sperm. The die is now cast. The unique order of genes is established and immutable. We are still to pass through the various stages of development, and be exposed to various influences of pregnancy, but the program for our development and characteristics is settled. The contract is signed! The sperm has merged with the egg.

Aldous Huxley put it thus: "A million, million spermatozoa all of them alive, out of their cataclysm but one poor Noah dare hope to survive; and of that billion minus one might have chanced to be Shakespeare, another

Newton, a new Dante; but the one was me. Shame to have ousted your betters thus, taking Ark while the others remained outside! Better for all of us, forward Homunculus (if you'd quietly died!)".

The same could be said of the ovum, each being unique. We are unique, immutable and special throughout our lives, rich or poor, big or small, smart or foolish. This specialness is established very early: at fertilization. What happens next is the "switching on" of the control system that will result in the development of the structure and form of the baby. The control system is the genes—the units of heredity, capable of replication, and transmitted from parent to offspring in the sperm and ovum.

The genes are carried on ribbon-like structures called chromosomes, which are contained in the head of the sperm and within the ovum; they come into contact and intermingle. Genes are structures of DNA, or deoxyribonucleic acid. There are at least 100,000 genes. The sequence of nitrogen bases along the two winding chains or coils that make up DNA establishes the code for the formation of proteins that ultimately determine not only structure and function but when such functions are "switched" on or off.

All the cells of the body contain these genes and chromosomes; they are found in a central structure called the nucleus, which directs the function of the cell. Humans have 46 chromosomes—23 pairs, including the X chromosome and the Y chromosome. We inherit half, or 23, of these unique and essential structures from each parent, but not before the genes along their lengths are shuffled like a pack of cards with those on each partner chromosome. The chromosomes contributed by our parents were in turn inherited from the grandparents. We are an amalgam of past generations—half of our parents, a quarter of each grandparent and so on.

This intermingling of material from both the sperm and ovum is the crucial event that determines our actual genetic endowment. The fertilized egg contains a combination of genes that is different from those of each parent, an arrangement unique for that person. Although the arguments rage about which side of the family our babies, children and we ourselves most resemble, the fact is that we are genetically half our mother and half our father.

These "immortal coils" of genes on the chromosomes are the basis for the continuing characteristics of all the living things on our planet. The great mystery at present is how these collections of genes along the coiled chromosomes put it all together, make an organism or a living, thinking and feeling being with desires, assertiveness and imagination—and soul.

Perhaps a clue lies in the discovery that these genes only comprise 4 percent of the length of the DNA and chromosomes. What is the function of the DNA that lies in between? Perhaps these structures enable the coordination of the genetic building blocks to construct the living being.

There is a prevalent belief, originating from the rigid scientific views of the Victorian era, that all human phenomena can be reduced to elementary responses which in turn can be reduced to physical and chemical scientific principles and laws. Known as Reductionism, it denies a place for values, meaning, purpose, spirit and soul. The genes are highly organized and directive, but do not impart higher order to the human race. How the animal or human displays its genetic endowment requires complex interaction with the environment. DNA are the building blocks from which our worldly house is constructed.

The "feel" of a house depends on the persons inhabiting it, the decoration and colour of the house, the aspect and position of the surrounding neighborhood, and the climate—and not just on the bricks, pipes, struts or tiles, or whether the faucets and switches work. Just as the house needs all these attributes, we, too, need to function well: this is essential. But many of our human attributes come from our experiences. Our bodily "house" has feeling, and lots of it!

There is now a substantial scientific basis for the fact that our fundamental behavior, reactions and attitudes—indeed our very spirit—can be changed by experience, particularly in regard to the brain and the senses before birth. The question to ask is not whether it occurs, but how much can be attributed to prenatal experience.

The Human Genome Project

A massive scientific undertaking has recently been organized: to map the whole of the DNA of the human—the controversial Human Genome Project. This is a scientific dream come true. Large groups of scientists and institutions are involved in this project, which is being organized on a chromosome by chromosome basis. Each of our 23 standard chromosomes and our sex chromosomes—the X and Y—are assigned to different scientific groups and institutions: there is a "centre for chromosome 22" and so on. The biochemical techniques are being automated. A complete map of our DNA is attainable, depending on technological and financial goals being fulfilled, perhaps within 10 years.

Interpreting the map will be the difficult task, particularly the interaction of various genes and the hundreds, perhaps thousands, of CPUs or central processing units which regulate the whole process—the promoters, enhancers and modulators, which often have multiple levels of complexity. It will provide information of great scientific value and will unlock many of the secrets of the body's chemistry.

Even with this information, it will not be possible to predict exactly the abilities, tendencies, creativeness and indeed the occurrence of many illnesses. The environmental perspective is important—our humanness is too individual, too unique to be definable in a test tube. The importance of experience in development should not be underestimated.

How Our Sex Is Determined

It is at the point of fertilization that our sex is determined, the sperm, and therefore the father, dictating what our sex will be. It is determined by a combination of the two so-called sex chromosomes, the X and the Y chromosome. Females have XX or two Xs and males are XY or an X and a Y. As the sperm and ovum each contain half of the chromosome or gene material, and the sex chromosomes pair and interact with each other, it can readily be seen that the female can only contribute an X and the male can contribute either an X or a Y, only one of which will be contained in any one sperm.

Fertilization of the ovum, containing an X, will either be by a sperm containing an X or a sperm containing a Y, to give a female (XX) or a male (XY). The Y chromosome is one of the smallest of the chromosomes and contains little genetic information except the ability to initiate the formation of the testis and initiate male sex hormone production (testosterone).

It is claimed by some that a couple can determine the sex of their offspring by the timing and management of intercourse. No one convincing method has been shown to be reliable and any gambler will indicate that a one in two chance will leave 50 percent of people satisfied and vocal about a method's success rate. Many couples have tried these methods and gone to special practitioners to learn them, emerging with reams of photocopied material which they usually follow very faithfully; the timing of intercourse, douching of the vagina and penetration instructions are followed "to the letter".

One couple with three boys were determined to have their girl. The instructions were followed exactly but, alas, a further boy was born. The father bought his distressed wife (or, if the truth be known, himself) a boat and duly named it *Amanda*. This couple are now delighted with their four boys and of course wouldn't have it any other way.

The desire to predict and influence the sex of the offspring is as old as human desire. In the 1st century AD, the Roman scribe Pliny gave a charming account of how Livia Augusta, the emperor Nero's wife, hatched a hen's egg in her bosom to find out if she was to have a boy or girl. The egg hatched a cock and, indeed, Livia Augusta gave birth to Tiberius Caesar.

Cultural, religious and economic issues have often led to attempts being made to influence the sex of the child, usually in favor of the male. Female infanticide after birth or detection of sex by modern prenatal diagnostic tests and termination of the female is apparently widely practiced in non-Western countries.

Mainland China pioneered some modern prenatal diagnostic tests in order to determine the sex of the single child and ensure that that child be male. In some parts of China this has resulted in disparate proportions of male and female children, there being about 120 male children to each 100 female. The social implications are likely to be considerable—many men will not be able to marry, due to the shortage of women.

A RAPID DEVELOPMENT

Once fertilization has taken place, the fertilized cell then divides. It will divide many, many times before birth, and in many cells the process continues for a lifetime. Until the moment our body stops, the journey is never complete. After the sperm has wooed its way to the outer two-thirds of the fallopian tube to fertilize the egg, or ovum, the embryo still has to journey back along the tube to become embedded in the womb (uterus).

The fertilized egg does not wait until it is established in the womb before starting its development. Rapid division occurs in the six or seven days it takes for the embryo to pass down and embed in the wall of the womb. Its passage down the tube is helped by muscular contractions of the tube that "milk" the rapidly dividing embryo towards the uterus or womb and a downstream current of mucus in the tube produced by the rhythmic and synchronized movement of hair-like cells on the wall of the tubes. First two, four, then eight cells, finally a ball of cells forms and then the layering of cells commences.

The developing cells undergo a complex series of specific changes to become the numerous organs of the body. Long before birth these organs will begin to function in the balanced way that is necessary to live successfully.

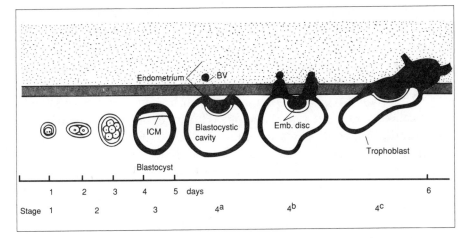

DEVELOPMENT OF *the embryo in the first week. Note that implantation in the uterus (womb) occurs after 5 days. BV = maternal blood vessel; ICM = inner cell mass, which forms the baby and the placenta (afterbirth). By Ronan O'Rahilly and Fabiola Muller, from* Human Embryology and Teratology, *Wiley Liss. Used with permission.*

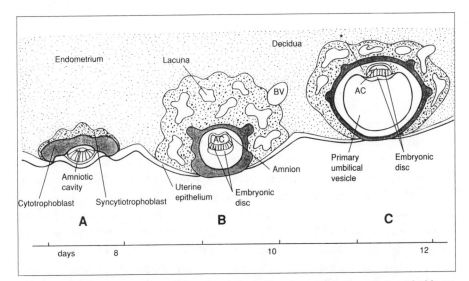

IMPLANTATION. *The embryo 'invades' the wall of the uterus. The placenta (trophoblast), at first solid, soon develops lacunae (cavities) which communicate with maternal blood vessels. AC = amniotic cavity ('Bag of waters'); BV = blood vessel. By Ronan O'Rahilly and Fabiola Muller, from* Human Embryology and Teratology, *Wiley Liss. Used with permission.*

This tiny living thing will be nourished by food supplied from the mother's body, but processed and distributed by its own life support system: the placenta. This growth and development is determined both by the environment provided within and without the mother's body, and by the genes that we inherited from both parents.

The embryo at 64 cells is a hollow ball with a concentration of 15 cells, the so-called inner cell mass, on one side. This inner cell mass contributes to the baby; the other cells form the tissues of the placenta and other surrounding and supportive structures. It has now been shown that only three cells of the inner cell mass actually contribute to the tissues of our body, i.e. three out of 64 cells. The early stages of the embryo at the four and eight cell stage can survive the removal of one or two cells and still produce a healthy infant animal as the cells are in such an early stage of development and appear to easily compensate fully for such a loss.

This is now being utilized in human embryos in some IVF programs to detect genetic abnormalities before replacing the embryo back into the recipient mother. One cell is removed and examined for some genetic conditions. The embryo will not suffer because of the removal of one cell. It can compensate for this loss. This ability to continue normal development despite removal of one cell is quickly lost once any structure or organ is formed.

TWINS AND MULTIPLE BIRTHS

Twins may originate from two ova or eggs, in which case they are non-identical or fraternal, or from one ovum if they are identical. Where splitting of the ovum takes place, this may occur in the first hours after fertilization or later, at about eight or nine days, just after implantation of the embryo into the wall of the uterus. Conjoined or Siamese twins occur when there is an attempt by the egg to split later, when we are just layers of cells and look like a plate or disc and before organs are formed. Conjoined twins can share legs, bowel, chest or heads. Most are lost as spontaneous abortions, but a few are born and some are able to be separated by modern surgical techniques.

Twins occur about one in every 90 pregnancies. However, with the advent of in vitro fertilization, and the placing of multiple ova in the womb, an increase in the incidence of multiple pregnancies has occurred in our community, especially the rare triplet and quadruplet births. Of course, all the IVF pregnancies are non-identical or fraternal—each ova and its sperm carry a different complement of its parent genes.

Two-thirds of spontaneous twins are non-identical. The frequency of identical twins is the same worldwide. Twins can run in families; the tendency for twins to recur, however, is only for non-identical twins. It is exclusively the mother who determines the tendency to have twins—the father's family history has *no* effect. It has also been found that if the firstborn are non-identical twins, the chance of the next pregnancy twinning is *five* times more likely to occur.

About one-third of fertilized ova do not implant in the uterus or womb and are lost. Of those that implant many have imperfections, especially in the number of chromosomes or genetic material, particularly an extra chromosome. Many are lost soon after implantation, even before the first missed period, so that the woman may never have known that she was pregnant. It has been estimated that due to some imperfection 60 percent of all conceptions or fertilized eggs do not go on to live birth.

Nature has its own way of filtering embryos and fetuses with defects—the spontaneous abortion. Even when miscarriages in the second and third trimesters of pregnancies, deaths in the womb or stillbirths occur, these have a high proportion of babies with severe defects. This has led to new concepts on the causation of birth defects; that they are a normal event in biology, a "blip" on the screen of normalcy, and that they are to be expected because the complexity of human development is such that mistakes are inevitable. Perhaps the 2 or 3 percent of live born babies who have defects are the milder end of a spectrum, or perhaps the mother is healthier and fitter and able to carry a baby with a defect to a live birth?

The struggle for life begins right from conception. Disease can alter structure and function and even cause demise very early.

2

From a Ball of Cells to a Human Image

The First Two Months

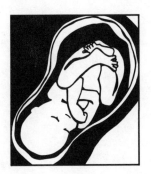

THE FIRST MONTH

Out of the unknown to a human image—this is the miraculous change that occurs during the first month of human life. We go from an ovum or egg so small as to be barely visible (about one 1/128th inch in diameter) to a young embryo two 1/100ths of an inch long that has increased 50 times in size and 40 thousand times in weight.

We change from a small round egg cell to a creature with a head, body and—it must be admitted—a tail, with a heart that beats, blood that circulates, the beginnings of arms, legs, eyes, ears, stomach and brain. In fact, during the first four weeks of our life almost every organ that serves us throughout our entire life has started to form. In addition to this astounding growth and development during this first month, we make our first struggle for food. For this purpose, we develop a special organ, the placenta, which enables us to draw food from our mother, allowing us to live a life of ease within the tissues of the uterus.

The rapidity of this first stage of development is staggering. The main activity after the embryo is lodged in the wall of the womb (called implantation) at seven to 14 days is the firm embedding of the embryo within the uterine wall. At this stage we are composed of two layers of cells in the form of flat sheets sandwiched to each other.

Real organ development starts during the third week after fertilization or the fifth week after the missed period. From now on, the exact age from fertilization will be our measure of age. This crucial third week after fertilization is when a third layer of cells is formed and when part of this top layer (or ectoderm) forms neural or nerve tissue destined to become the brain and the spinal cord. At this stage we are still flattened layers of cells, called descriptively a disc. However, head and tail ends, left and right and top and bottom can be distinguished.

At the end of the third week, the real business of forming organs commences. We should take a moment to reflect that in the short period from the end of the third week to the end of the eighth week, or six weeks after the last missed period, we develop from the embryonic disc to a fully formed human embryo/fetus, which is recognizable as a human by the facial and body structure, has a beating heart and formed limbs, and has started to move and breathe the surrounding fluid.

The significant event in the establishment of general body form is the folding of the flat disc into a somewhat cylindrical embryo. It folds either side to form the "cylinder" and also folds lengthwise. The rate of growth is greater lengthwise, and there is a buckling at the top and bottom ends—our head and bottom ends. Incredibly, the heart begins its development at the top of the disc, but because of the buckling and folding finds itself below the top end, abutting against the disc, the lateral sides of the embryo folding around it to form the chest.

After the longitudinal and lateral folding, the attachment of the embryo to the placenta is formed: the umbilical cord.

The embryo heart begins to beat at about the 24th day, or about five weeks after the last period, and, for the remaining eight months before birth and the 60–90 years of independent life after birth, the heart must continue to beat. Once the heart starts beating on the 24th day after fertilization the life of the individual depends on its continuous, steady, rhythmic beating.

The heart is still just a long tube. It has to develop into its various chambers and develop valves, all of which are complete by the end of the eighth week. However, this first beating and rhythmic expanding and contracting so impressed philosophers and scientists of early times that they believed that this miracle of the tiny heart beating in an otherwise very simple embryo was the moment when the vital spark of life, the spirit or soul, entered the body. One has sympathy with this notion, especially as the ancient philosophers considered that the heart was the seat of the soul and emotion, and that the lung tubes that passed over it connected the heart to the voice box, giving rise to vented emotions in language.

The time when the organs are forming is, despite our tiny size, a critical period for the embryo. If this normal sequence of organ formation is

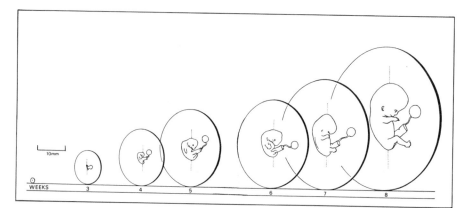

RELATIVE SIZES *of embryo, chorion, and yolk sac from conception until 56 days. From O'Rahilly (Developmental Stages in Human Embryos, Carnegie Institution of Washington, Publication 631, 1973). Used with permission.*

disturbed even slightly, the effect will magnify progressively as growth and development proceed. Any factor which can cause birth defects will have its greatest effect during this period, as only a tiny change in sequence development can give rise to the malformation of an organ.

An added problem is that often the mother does not know or appreciate she is pregnant until after the first and second missed periods, equivalent to two and six weeks after fertilization. Usually she does not confirm the pregnancy until the second missed period. By that time most of the organs have completed their development. Until such time as she is aware of her pregnancy, she will not know to take any special care. Exposure to infections such as German measles or rubella and drugs such as thalidomide have their major effect during this time.

During the fourth week of life the human embryo continues its rapid development, tripling its size in seven days. At this stage, the embryo of many animal species such as the chicken, the rat, the elephant and the chimpanzee look very similar to that of the human. In the time from the fourth to the eighth week we make our change from a nondescript tadpole-like structure to one which has a distinctly human appearance and can be recognized immediately as human and not as any other animal. The unmistakable human features of the face are present, though it is rather grotesque, with a very large head and forehead, small chin and nose—not unlike E.T.! The head, containing the most complex and continually developing organ, the brain, is the largest structure in the body, making up one-quarter of its length.

THE SECOND MONTH

The human face is built up gradually around the wide mouth. The first step is the formation of the lower jaw at about the fifth week, the upper jaw forming and fusing on the sixth week. Failure of these upper jaw bars to fuse will cause a cleft of the upper lip in the newborn baby. Therefore, clefts of the lip and face result from the failure of *normal* structures to fuse, not an aberration or monstrosity in development. The eyes are bulging and situated on the side of the head, and the nose is formed of two pits, which correspond to the nasal cavities. These nasal pits gradually move around to the front as the embryo increases rapidly in size. At around the seventh week the eyelids form, closing down the eyes for the following four months of life. Premature babies cannot open their eyes until 24 weeks. And so we have the human face, a tiny

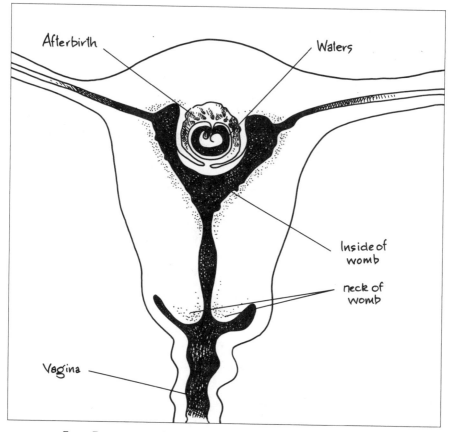

AT 6 WEEKS. *From* Pregnancy and Birth, *New South Wales Department of Health. Used with permission.*

small lower jaw and chin, a tiny pug nose, eyes far apart and a bulging head and brain. Nevertheless, it is fully recognizable as human.

Another feature which makes the seven or eight week embryo human-like is that the limbs have now developed. At the end of the first month our limbs are purely buds, sprouting out from the body. Firstly the upper limb buds are formed and then the lower limb buds. Therefore the arm begins and completes each successive stage of development earlier than those of the leg. About the fifth week there is a good length of limb and the end is now forming a paddle-like ridge which is the hand or foot plate.

How does the fetus decide which end of the hand is the thumb, and which end to put the little finger? Researchers have made the surprising discovery that the substance that determines the order of hand structures is retinoic acid, a derivative of vitamin A. Retinoic acid is produced within the embryo, being switched on at the crucial time to form a gradient across the hand and foot. This gradient dictates the position of the thumb, which corresponds to a high concentration of vitamin A, and the little finger corresponds to a lower concentration of this remarkable compound.

Vitamin A is an essential vitamin—we get much of it by eating sources of beta carotene, the compound that makes carrots and pumpkins orange and lobsters red. Retinoic acid also appears to be important in the development of parts of the brain and spinal column, the face, heart, skeleton, liver and the skin. Vitamin A, as an essential vitamin for infant and adult life, remains important after birth in controlling the growth and health of epithelial or surface tissue, which consists of the skin, breast, lung lining, intestines and other organs. Too much vitamin A can be quite dangerous, with doses 10 times normal actually causing birth defects (see chapter on Practical Applications).

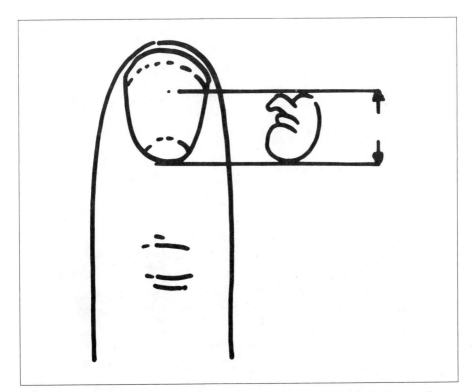

AT 6 WEEKS *the fetus is about 5mm long, or a bit smaller than your little fingernail, from its head to its bottom.*

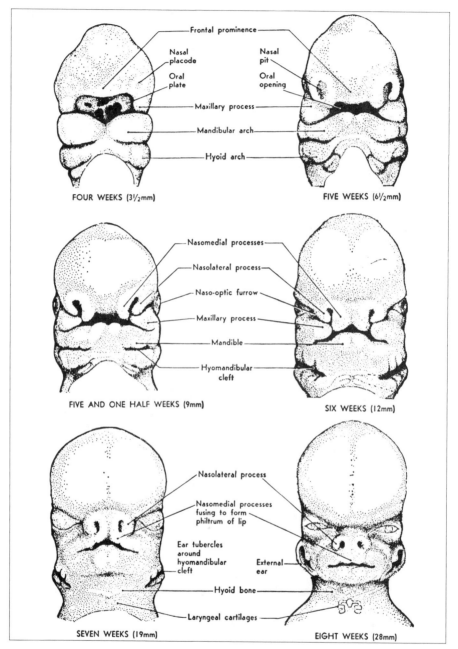

FRONTAL APPEARANCE *of developing craniofacies from days 28–56 (ovulation age).*
Drawn from embryos in the Carnegie Collection by Patten (Human Embryology, *ed.*
3, McGraw-Hill Book Co., 1968). Used with permission.

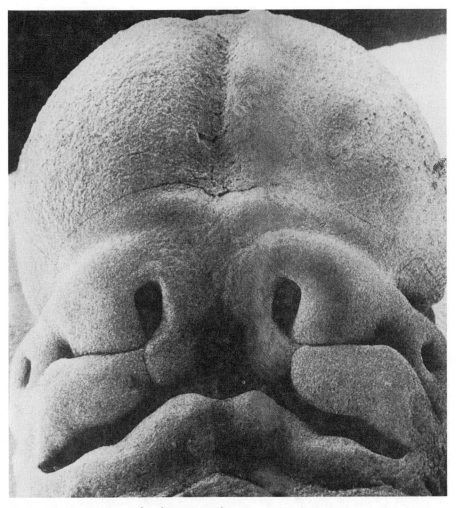

THE HUMAN FACE *at six weeks after conception.*

Five parallel ridges separated by narrow grooves appear within each hand and foot plate. The cells that are forming the grooves or webs undergo "death" or degeneration to separate the fingers and toes. Cell death as well as cell growth is already an important part of human development. The webbed feet of the duck are the result of a failure of degeneration of the web between the toes that is present in all of us at this early stage.

The importance of this so-called "programmed" cell death is now appreciated in the formation of all organ systems, including that of the brain.

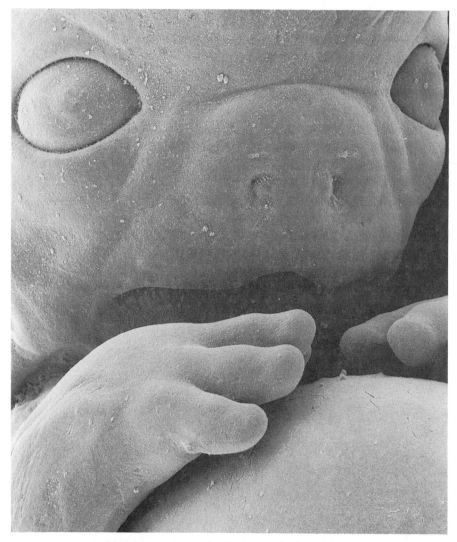

THE HUMAN FACE *and hands at eight weeks. Professor Kathy Sulik, Birth Defects Center, The University of North Carolina. Used with permission.*

Without programmed or structured cell death we would be a very different-looking animal indeed. Cell death sculptures some structures, rounds off edges, separates and gets rid of unwanted tissue. The fetus is forever changing its structure and form in a supreme adaptation to both its environment and its development. Death as well as growth is part of normal development.

By the seventh week, nail beds are forming; the true horny nails do not develop until the fifth month. During the same period the elbow, knee, wrist and ankle are formed. Bones and muscles develop within the arms and legs. It is not until the end of the second month that the legs become longer than the arms. The foot plates originally face each other, sole facing sole, but now they have rotated so the knees face up and the soles downwards. From this time on, throughout the fetal period, childhood and adolescence, the legs represent an increasingly greater proportion of the total length of the human.

The development of muscle also proceeds at a startling pace. By the end of the second month all the large muscles typical of the human body have developed, forming a thick blanket of padding between the skin and the underlying bones. The original continuous blanket of muscle separates rapidly to make distinct muscles.

The definitive pattern is present by the end of the second month, and at this stage the embryo starts moving. Yes, moving, firstly as jerky uncoordinated movements and then assuming specific movements of the arms and legs. Our philosophers may ponder that this first sign of activity, unable to be felt by the mother because of the cushioning of the fluid surrounding the baby and the muscle of the uterus, may be the first sign of activity typical of a living man or woman.

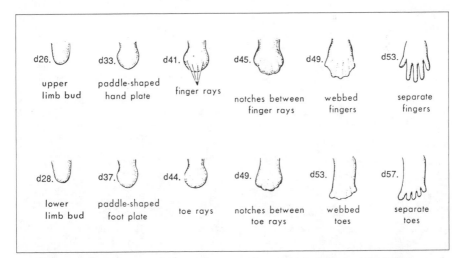

FORMATION OF HANDS, *days 26-53, and feet, days 28-57. From Roman O'Rahilly,* Developmental Stages in Human Embryos, *Carnegie Institution of Washington, Publication 631, 1973, and Keith L. Moore,* The Developing Human, *ed. 4, W.B. Saunders Co., 1988. Used with permission.*

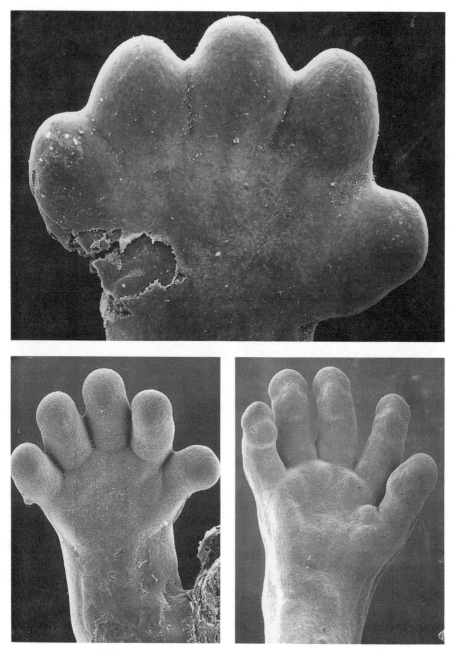

DEVELOPMENT OF *the hand: top, 7 weeks; left, 7½ weeks; right, 9 weeks. Professor Kathy Sulik, Birth Defects Center, The University of North Carolina, and the Proceedings of the Greenwood Genetic Center, Volume 11. Used with permission.*

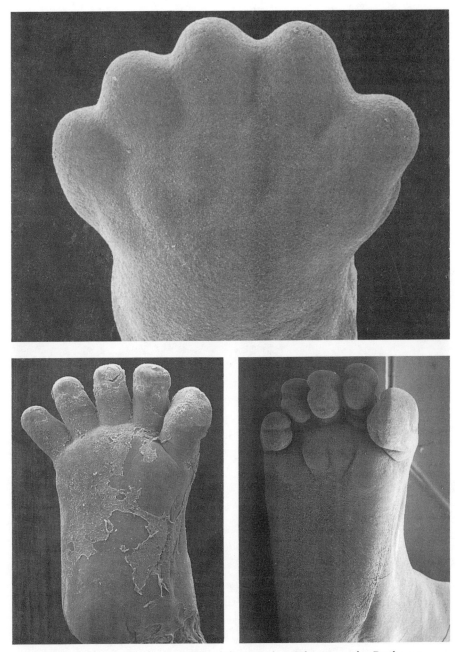

DEVELOPMENT OF *the foot: top, 7½ weeks; left, 8 weeks; right, 10 weeks. Professor Kathy Sulik, Birth Defects Center, The University of North Carolina, and the Proceedings of the Greenwood Genetic Center, Volume 11. Used with permission.*

So the second month of life closes with a stamp of human likeness clearly imprinted on the embryo. All the organs that will serve us during our life have progressed very far on in their development. So completely is the fundamental plan achieved that the biologist marks this as the end of the embryonic period. Henceforth, we are called a fetus. Our transition from an egg to embryo to the beginning of the fetus has now been initiated.

Antonj Van Leeuwenhoek, the Dutch draper who invented the microscope, noted the beginning of the fetal period in 1683 thus: "The human foetus tho no bigger than a GREEN PEA, yet is furnished with all its parts".

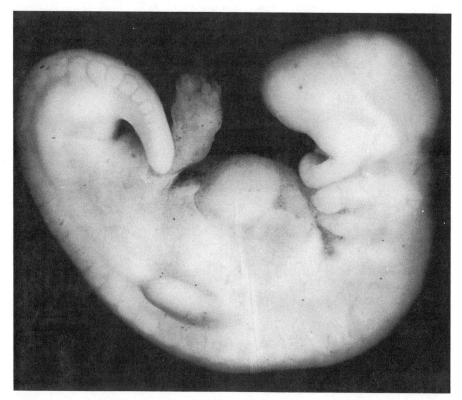

THE HUMAN *embryo at 28 days post conception. Note that the upper limb bud is present but not the lower. The heart has started to beat at 24 days. The curled tail is characteristic at this stage, as are the pharyngeal arches which form the face and the umbilical cord. Congenital Anomaly Research Center, Kyoto University, Faculty of Medicine. Used with permission.*

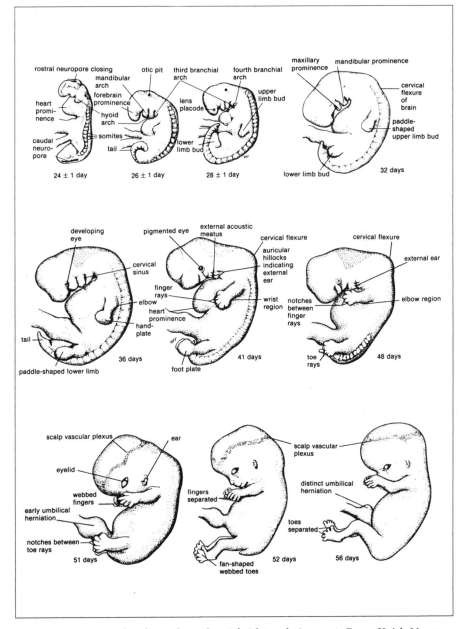

LATERAL APPEARANCE *of embryos from days 24-56 (ovulation age). From Keith Moore,* **Before We Are Born,** *ed. 3, W.B. Saunders and Co., 1988. Used with permission.*

A truly magnificent feat of biology, the development of the embryo and fetus, is now well advanced. Most organs have either formed or are well on the way. The most notable exceptions are the brain, which continues its development right through the pregnancy, and the genital or external sex organs, which have only just passed beyond the neuter stage and are extremely difficult to distinguish between male and female. At the end of the eighth week the fetus is only ¾ of an inch long, but has grown massively from the ⅟₁₆th of an inch at the end of the third week. You, the reader, have now had your first glimpse into that interesting world, the life that occurs before birth.

3

Maturation, Growth and Practice

From Three to Nine Months

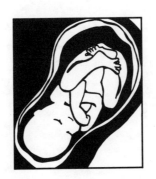

Now the fetus commences a seven month period of maturation, practice and perfection called the fetal stage. Why does the human have such a long period in the womb of the mother? In some animals, the young are born at much earlier stages in their development. For example, the possum gives birth to her offspring when they are barely as mature as a two-month human embryo; the newborn mouse and rat are blind, hairless and helpless creatures, little better prepared for independent life than the four month old human. In most other animals, the young are very mature at birth: for instance, the horse can stand up and walk almost immediately after birth.

The long gestation and the relative immaturity of the human has evoked a lot of speculation amongst scientists and anthropologists. One conclusion is that the very advanced final development of the human needs a more complex and larger brain. The human brain takes longer to develop, with locomotion and language not developing before the end of the first year, or 21 months after conception. The human, it can be argued, compared to animals, is born nearly one year too early.

As well as attaining the erect posture by adaptation of the pelvic shape to the mechanical requirements of an upright posture, the relative size of the brain is increased in the human, compared to the animal species. The human head size at one year of age would be too big to fit through the mother's birth canal (the bony ring above the hips called the pelvis). Even to fit through at nine months after conception, the human fetal head must rotate through at least a quarter turn or 90°, sometimes as much as 180°, and the head is normally compressed during the process of birth, the bones of the skull having fibrous hinges or sutures which can accommodate compression and shape changes. Anthropologists have speculated that this large head size resulted in an obstetric or birth and delivery dilemma which could only be resolved by shortening the duration of pregnancy and this naturally resulted in the birth of a less mature human newborn.

FETAL MOVEMENT

The first movements of the fetus appear to be largely spontaneously generated and do not need external control from the mother, either mechanically or from hormones. The importance of these movements in normal development is now starting to be appreciated. If the muscles do not contract and move the limbs, they waste and become scarred. If the joints do not move, they seize up. These movements are important in the development of the nervous system as, to a certain extent, the pattern of the nervous connections within the brain and spinal cord are determined by these movements. The useless nerve cells and connections which do not participate, degenerate.

An interesting category of fetal movements are those which anticipate postnatal functions, for instance, the movements of breathing. Of course, there is no air to breathe in the womb; the fetus breathes the fluid in the fluid bag which surrounds the baby (the amniotic fluid). As with the beating of the heart, the fetus starts the breathing movements very early in gestation, at 10 weeks after conception, and these movements will never stop until the day this person dies. But in fetal breathing there is no intake or transference of oxygen—so why breathing movements?

Further examination indicates a very important function. The muscles of the diaphragm, the sheet of muscle at the bottom of the lung that separates it from the abdomen and the rib muscles, are essential for breathing; they need to be given practice and require movement in order to develop. It has also been shown that the maturation of lung tissue needs these movements. The most remarkable fact is the onset of the so-called respiratory reflexes such as yawns and stretches. This remarkable lifelong invariance seems astonishing considering the immaturity of the brain and spinal cord at the commencement of these movements at 10–12 weeks.

These fetal breathing movements are by no means an exception, as the fetal eyes start to move at 16–18 weeks, before exposure to the light of the world. Like the muscles of the limbs and the chest, the muscles of the eyes need practice, presumably so that their neurone or nerve cell connections are correctly made, and the muscles are conditioned at birth. These movements are spontaneously generated and only later are associated with visual stimuli.

Movements of the fetus are also important in shaping and strengthening the bones. If the fetus does not move vigorously in the womb, not only do the muscles waste away and degenerate but also there are vast changes in the bones. They become thinner, brittle and more liable to break. The actual growth and shape of the bones themselves is also compromised.

The use of ultrasound and its potential for direct observation have shed light on these rather remarkable facts. Ultrasound was developed in the 1970s and early 80s as a non-invasive technique to produce an image of internal organs and, of course, the fetus. Similar to echoes and radar, high frequency sound waves are transmitted and reflected off internal structures, and a picture of the organs or baby can be viewed on a TV screen. The "sounds" cannot be heard as they are much too high in frequency—hence "ultrasound".

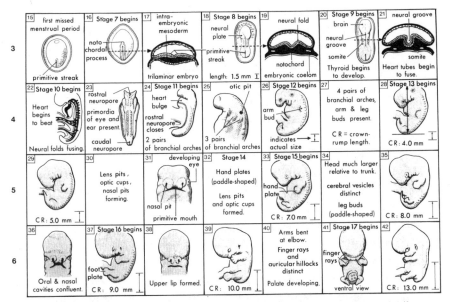

THE MAIN *features of developmental stages in human embryos are illustrated. The weeks are given on the left and the days at the top left corners. From Keith L. Moore,* The Developing Human, *W.B. Saunders and Co., 1988. Used with permission.*

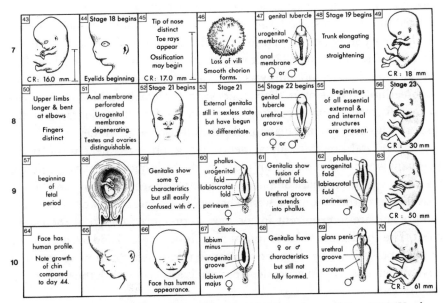

FROM KEITH *L. Moore,* The Developing Human, *W.B. Saunders and Co., 1988. Used with permission.*

A different wave length is used with radar. The quality and definition of the images have improved dramatically over the last 10 years—so has the complexity and expense of the ultrasound machines.

Connection to a printer and image maker will produce still pictures and connection to a video recorder will record movements. Even the movement of blood in the heart and vessels can be imaged in colour, depending on whether the blood is flowing towards or from the ultrasound source or sensor.

Utilization of the Doppler technique (named after the Austrian physicist Christian Johann Doppler) can detect speed, wave form and pressure within blood vessels. The Doppler technique is also used in police radar traps to determine accurate speeds of the motor car. This phenomenon also explains why a train whistle appears to change note: an approaching train has a higher note and a lower note as it moves away. The speed of the train determines the pitch of the note.

Perhaps even more remarkable is the level of knowledge about fetal movements present a century ago before the systematic study afforded by ultrasound of the fetus. A German physiologist, Dr N.T. Preyer, described in 1872 the onset of motility thus: "The fetus moves its arms and legs long before the beginning of the 16th week, probably long before the 12th week". (We now know the onset is at seven and a half weeks.) Dr Preyer also realized that the fetus drank the fluid in the bag of water (amniotic fluid).

The existence of human fetal breathing movements was also recognized by a Dr Ahlfeld in 1888, but was rejected by scientists of the Edwardian period. It was felt that not only was the fetus stuporous, it was also apnoeic, or not breathing. It took more than eighty years for fetal breathing movements to be rediscovered and to become a hobby-horse for ultrasonographers, the doctors who monitor and diagnose by the ultrasound machines.

The fetal breathing movements can be observed near term in the pregnant woman. If one carefully observes the belly button or navel region of a woman who is pregnant and near term, one may see fine rising and falling movements of the abdominal wall. They occur at a rate of between 60–80 per minute and are intermittent in the most pronounced region of the child's chest. The child's rate of breathing at birth is between 30 and 60, decreasing to 7–12 per minute by the time adulthood is reached. Brain wave readings have shown that a brain wave sleep pattern is associated with the more rapid respirations.

The growth of the baby in the womb is obvious from just simple observation of the mother. The maturation aspects of the baby, in particular the necessity to practice and affirm aspects of development, are not obvious.

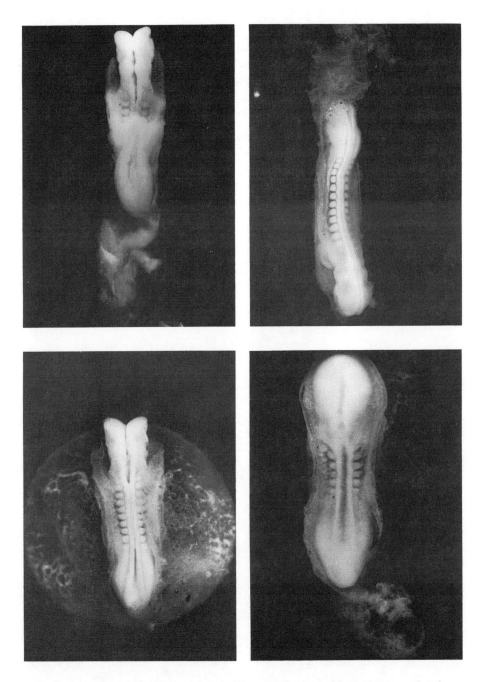

EARLY HUMAN *embryos, less than 26 days. The neural tube and brain have not fused. Congenital Anomaly Research Center, Kyoto University, Faculty of Medicine. Used with permission.*

If the baby in the womb cannot move, breathe and interact with its environment it will suffer physical and mental deterioration that at the very least will temporarily, and at the worst permanently, affect development. Its life and movement before birth is crucial in shaping the life after birth. Child developmentalists over the past 40 years have realized the importance of movement, practice, stimulation and interaction for the normal development of the baby and young child. Appreciation of just such stimulation before birth is just as, or perhaps more important for normal fetal development.

4

The Development of Sex

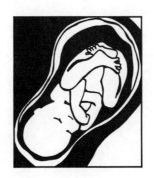

Although it is determined and programmed from fertilization whether a person will be male or female, it is not possible to distinguish the sex of the developing embryo/fetus, except by direct examination of the sex chromosomes, until after the sixth or seventh week and then it is only possible by careful examination of the internal sex organ or gonad under the microscope to distinguish whether it is a testis or an ovary. Until the ninth week the external sex organs or genitals of the two sexes look the same.

The primitive "germ" cells which eventually grow and change to form eggs or sperm pass from a sac-like structure called the "yolk sac" on the underside of the embryo to the back of the abdominal cavity. Here they form bulges on both sides associated with the developing kidneys. During the seventh week either the inner part of these bulges starts to be recognizable as a testicle or the outer part will go on in the next few weeks to develop into an ovary. Therefore, at the heart of every (fetal) ovary, there lies an undeveloped testis.

Descriptions of the development of the sex organs as being originally female and then developing into a male are just not right. We are originally neuter or sexless and "indifferent". Externally it is impossible to tell man from woman up to at least 12 weeks and internally up to seven weeks.

This means that for every female genital structure, there is a corresponding male structure, and for every male genital structure, there is a corresponding female structure. For instance, the penis corresponds to the clitoris, which has the same structures, though it is much smaller, and doesn't have a urethra or urine tube through the middle of it. It has a tip and a shaft and becomes engorged with blood and erect with stimulation and sexual excitement. Even at 15 weeks the clitoris is the same size as the penis. The bag which holds the testicles in the male, called the scrotum, develops from the same structure that the labia majora or the outer folds around the opening to the vagina develop. The inner folds or labia minora fuse together in the male to form the urethra or urine tube in the penis. Amazingly, within every male there is a rudimentary vagina, cervix and uterus and within every female there is a duct system, similar to the ejaculatory ducts of the male testis, that drains the ovary, albeit very degenerate and useless.

The signal that initiates the development of the male results in the secretion of the male hormone testosterone, as well as a hormone that causes regression of the female ducts and structures. The genes that switch on this signal at six to seven weeks are present in both the X and Y chromosome. Remember the female has two X chromosomes—XX, and the male one X

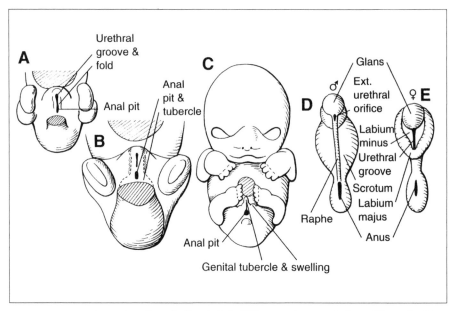

DEVELOPMENT OF *the external genitalia. A-C, indifferent phase at 5, 6, and 7 weeks. D and E, male and female genitalia at 10 weeks (60 mm). From* Human Embryology and Teratalogy, *R. O'Rahilly and F. Muller—Wiley Liss. Used with permission.*

and one Y—XY. As only one X is active in the female, the signal is twice as strong in the male. It is not the absence or presence of the gene or signal but the dose that is significant—the similarity of the male and female are that close. Regardless of the number of X chromosomes, embryos with a Y chromosome develop as males.

Geneticists have shown that only a tiny section of the Y chromosome, probably 1 percent, possesses the special signal to switch on the gonad in the male to develop into a testis, produce testosterone and thus to develop to a male. It is called appropriately the testis determining factor (TDF). Remember that the female has an identical gene on the X chromosome. A double dose is needed to develop a testis. This gene is evolutionarily conserved. That is, it is the same gene in most mammals.

The gonads descend from the back of the abdomen during the fetal period. The ovary reaches its position just below the pelvic bone at 12 weeks and the testis the inside of the groin by 28 weeks. The testicles then descend from the groin to the scrotum, reaching it in four weeks or by 32 weeks or eight months. They may be delayed and descend in the first months or years after birth. The testicles need to be in the scrotum to complete their maturation and finally form sperm themselves. A strange situation for such an essential and sensitive organ! The sperm cells can only mature, it seems, at a temperature that is 2–5° F below that of the body, and thus are situated externally, away from the warmth of the abdomen.

The testosterone that is produced in the first trimester not only achieves the transformation of the genitals into male organs, but it also organizes corresponding male behavior early in life. As with the genitals, the female pattern of behavior develops in the absence of the masculinizing hormonal influence. For instance, in rats with functional male genitals who are deprived of male sex hormone immediately after birth (corresponding to the end of the second trimester in the human), male sexual behavior such as mounting will be reduced and replaced by female sexual behavior such as receptive or female mating posture in *adulthood*. Anatomical differences in the hypothalamus, the area of the brain that organizes male and female reproductive behavior and is situated under the frontal lobe of the brain, have been shown in both experimental animals and the human.

Now, with the exception of sex chromosomes, men and women share the same genetic material. It was at first thought that the functional potential of the male and female brains were identical, and that the marked differences in function were due to societal, sociological and historical influences on the way that little boys and little girls are treated. It is true that the environment in such a sophisticated animal as the human has enormous influence, and society's expectations cannot be ignored. But recent research, particularly by the controversial Professor Doreen Kimura of the University of Western Ontario in Canada, has found definite functional and problem solving differences between the sexes that cannot be explained by environment alone.

The sex differences in brain function lie in abilities rather than overall level of intelligence. Men are, on the average, better at some special tasks such as tests that require the subject to imagine rotating an object or manipulating it. Again men are better, on the average, in mathematical reasoning tests and navigating their way through a route. The sexist jibes about women having a weaker ability with the route map may have some basis in fact. Men are also more accurate in tests of target-directed motor skills—darts, archery and ball sports.

But hold on! The men can't get too carried away with these skills. Women are better at rapidly identifying matching items—called perceptual speed—have greater verbal fluency and find the right words or words beginning with a specific letter. Women can also outperform men in arithmetic calculation and in recalling landmarks from a route, and are faster at precision manual tasks.

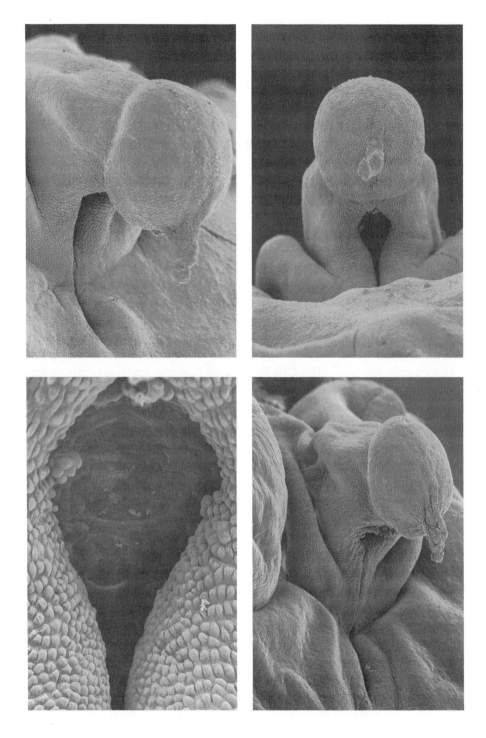

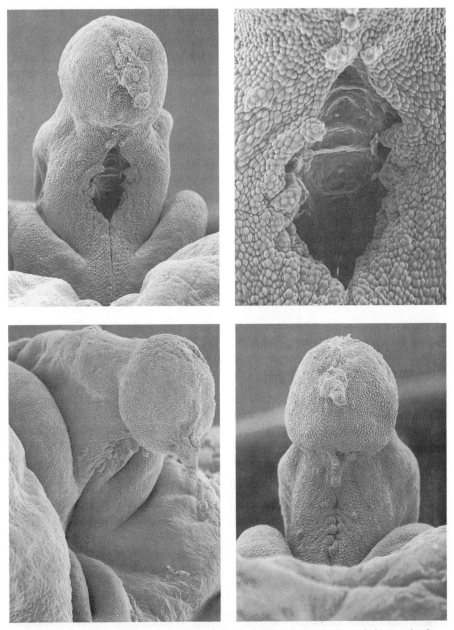

DEVELOPMENT OF *the genitals at 57 days, showing stages in the fusion of the urethral (urine tube) folds. Professor Kathy Sulik, Birth Defects Center, the University of North Carolina. From the Proceedings of the Greenwood Genetic Center, Volume 8. Used with permission.*

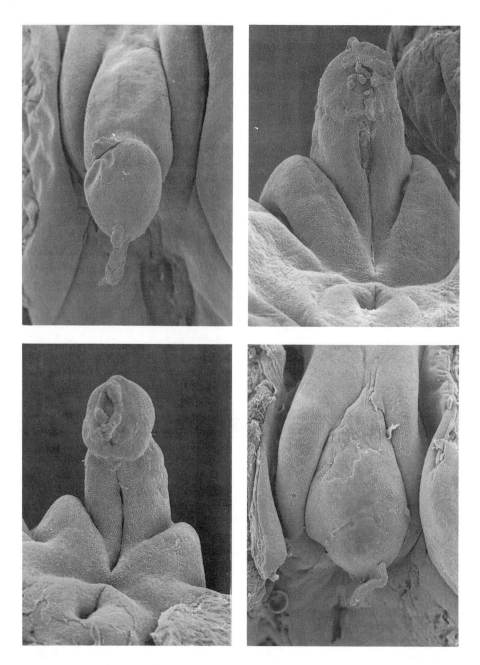

DEVELOPMENT OF *the genitals in female and male. Professor Kathy Sulik, Birth Defects Center, the University of North Carolina. From the Proceedings of the Greenwood Genetic Center, Volume 8. Used with permission.*

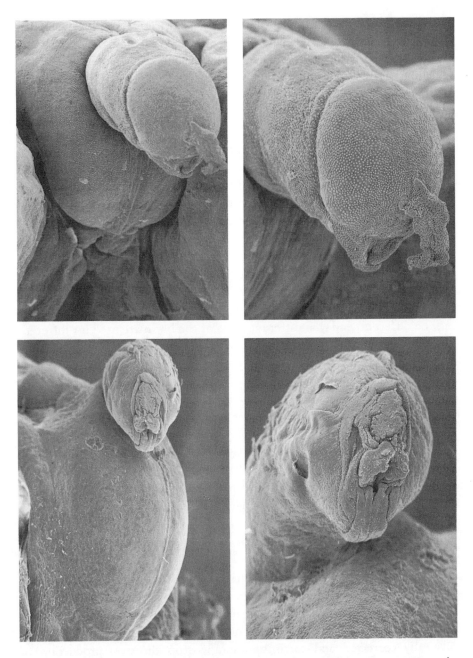

Opposite: Female human fetus at 11 weeks showing clitorus. This page, top: 11 week old male; bottom: 14 week old male. Note the growth of the foreskin.

There is a clang of recognition in these differences, even when one discards the sexist labels. These are tightly grouped averages only. There will be macho men better than many women in precision manual tasks and perceptual speed and sensual women better than many men in navigating and mathematical reasoning. The various attributes of the male and female appear to be present before puberty, and probably have their origins in fetal development.

Professor Kimura found that different parts of the brain are used for speech and movement in the female compared to the male. Under the influence of hormones, function is different, but structure is probably the same in male and female. Why "probably"? Well, scientists have found differences in some animals. For instance, the song center in the male canary is larger, and it can sing more complex songs as a result. This effect is due to the male sex hormone testosterone acting on the brain's development.

The evidence for such differences between the sexes in the human is controversial. Some research, including that of Professor Kimura, has indicated that the lining between the nerve cells in the male and female brain may be different, and that different parts of the brain are used for different functions in the sexes. For example, the front area of the brain seems more important for speech in females than males, and may underlie the woman's superior verbal abilities.

Rare and unusual mistakes of nature can provide us with vital clues. If a baby's sex is mistaken at birth—if there are "ambiguous" genitals and a boy is thought to be a girl at birth, is given a girl's name and brought up as a girl—that person will usually have a firm sex of assignment, despite the genetic constitution of a sex opposite to that which the person has positively adopted. Our parenting and societal practices have adapted that person's behavior and desires. Psychologists have firmly indicated that such children should continue in their selected sex and have surgery to make the change. Attempts to change back to the genetic sex in the past have resulted in major psychiatric illness and confusion.

Some of the babies in this group have the condition called congenital adrenal hyperplasia or CAH. Due to a birth defect in the production of sex hormone, girls with this condition are exposed to excessive male hormone or testosterone. Although the subsequent abnormality of the genitals can be surgically corrected and cortisone therapy stop the over-production of testosterone, effects of prenatal exposure on the brain may not be reversed. For example, girls with CAH treated in the first weeks after birth grow up to be more tomboyish and aggressive.

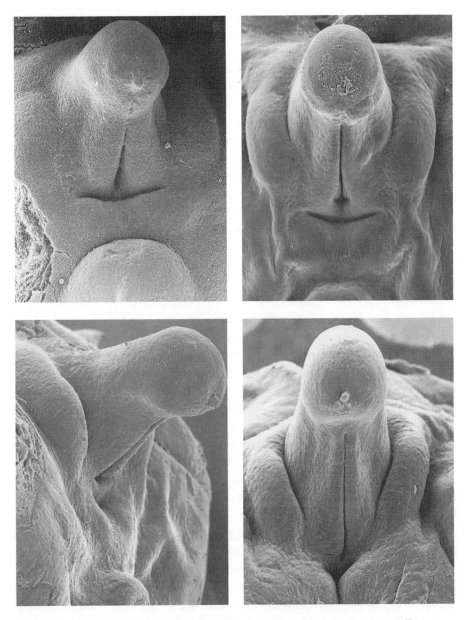

DEVELOPMENT OF *the genitals in the eighth week. Note the formation of a phallus (penis or clitorus). The vertical slit fuses in the male to form the urethra—the tube through which the urine flows. The horizontal slit is the anus. Professor Kathy Sulik, Birth Defects Center, the University of North Carolina. From the Proceedings of the Greenwood Genetic Center, Volume 8. Used with permission.*

Of course, expectation can be difficult to rule out in such studies, which have been based on interviews and teacher ratings. Expectation on the part of the adults who knew the girls' history or even from the girls themselves may have caused the results. Play behavior such as toy preference is also different and male-orientated in the treated CAH girls. In other studies, the known male tasks such as spatial ability and manipulation are performed better in the females with CAH. This and other scientific work has suggested strongly that the male and female brain are organized on different lines from very early in life. During development, including development before birth, the sex hormones may direct such differences.

Over tens of thousands of years we evolved as hunter gatherers, in small groups. The division of tasks between men and women in these ancient societies was very marked. Men were responsible for hunting game and travelling large distances. Evolutionary pressure to better route-finding ability and targeting skills would be operative. Women gathered food near the camp, prepared food and clothing and cared for children. Likewise evolutionary pressures would be towards short-range navigation using landmarks and fine motor capabilities in a circumscribed space.

Professor Kimura affirms that we need to look beyond the demands of modern life to seek the reason for these differences between the sexes. We did not undergo natural selection for reading and operating computers. The findings of consistent sex differences, initiated early in life and indeed before birth, and independent of societal influences is an important concept, and should not be treated with derision or contempt, but with respect. Acceptance of the differences, building on the strengths inherent in being male and female, is important in determining our individual uniqueness.

New scientific studies have shown another fascinating effect of sex on our genetic inheritance: some genes depend on the sex of the parent to determine how they will affect the structure and function of the offspring. This remarkable and rather surprising effect, known as imprinting, is important in all mammals and the human. We need the functional presence of genes from both a male and a female to imprint and function and even sometimes to ensure survival. These genes and their chromosomes are separate from the sex chromosomes, but somehow the complementary aspects of genes that need to pair up from our mother and our father are necessary to ensure normalcy—a remarkable but apparently important genetic concept.

In lower and primitive life forms it is possible for the life form to complete development without a contribution of the male by duplication of the genes in the egg. A female would result. This is not possible in the human due to imprinting: the egg will not survive as it has a duplication of genes and chromosomes from the female. At present the actual effect of imprinting is only known in disease states: some diseases are expressed differently depending on the sex of the transmitting parent. For example, in Huntingtons disease the age of onset of this late, debilitating dementia is earlier if the father rather than the mother transmitted the disease. Fascinating questions immediately arise: "What normal functions and characteristics are dependent on imprinting?". Are some physical characteristics or even temperament only able to be inherited from the mother, and others only able to be inherited from the father? The next few years may give us answers to these intriguing questions.

Psychoanalytical theory talks about the masculine in woman, the animus, and the feminine in man, the anima, indicating that it is important to recognise the opposite sex in our psychological selves and development. This journey together provides enrichment and enlargement of life for the individual and a rich partnership of the human spirit. Knowledge of our fetal development is confirmatory, as we always retain our maleness and femaleness in our structural body, indeed in our brain as well. Our original potentials were the same, in a physiological and anatomical sense! One gene determines the difference. However, whether we feel or think of the animus and anima within ourselves, the physical presence of the opposite sex remains with us for a lifetime.

5

The Remarkable Organ That Makes Us Human

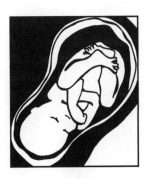

The brain and the nervous system (the nerves, spinal cord and the sense organs such as the eyes, internal ear and the organs of touch, taste and smell) are incredibly complex. An adult human brain has more than 100 *billion* nerve cells. They are connected by millions of "wires" or axons in a complex and unique way so that they can direct movement, the senses, speech, feeling and, most importantly, memory, learning experience, inspiration and spirit. This computer is not just switched on at birth. It is operative well before birth. The wiring is not completed by a predetermined computer-like chip. In order to complete the complex development necessary the brain must be stimulated and from such stimulation at all levels the structure of the cells and wiring are sculpted.

The brain is the most complex organ in the human body and this complexity is reflected in the fact that although it is the first body organ to begin its development (18 days), it is the last system to reach functional maturity (four years). The brain is the largest organ of the embryonic body; at nine weeks its size is 25 percent of the total body. As the fetus forms and grows the brain comprises a progressively smaller part in the total body size and after birth it continues to decrease its relative size to 10 percent of the total body weight in the newborn infant and only 2 percent of the total body weight of the adult.

Within the brain, the greatest and the most complex growth occurs in the hemispheres, the two symmetrical and balloon-like structures on each side of the midline at the very top of the brain. These cerebral hemispheres with the outer "grey matter" (the nerve cells) and the inner "white matter" (the connecting fibers) are the most distinctive and elaborately developed organ in the human body and the prime factor in the difference and apparent superiority of humans to other animals.

The brain starts its development as a layer of cells called the neural plate on the upper part of the embryonic "disc" at 18 days. By 23 days this plate has formed a tube. By different rates of growth, which cause flexing and folding, this tube becomes expanded and more complex at the top (the brain) and thinner and longer in the lower half (the spinal cord).

After the cells have completed their development at the age of four or five, no further increase in nerve cells of the brain occurs and in general, nerve cells cannot regenerate in the way that a cut on the skin can heal, so that if injury or disease occurs, the cells will not reform and grow as with a skin wound. Adaptation can however result in a meaningful and apparently complete recovery in function, as some functions can be taken over by other parts of the brain. The covering of the wires or axons is still not fully developed until adolescence so that the microvolt electricity that powers our brain moves slower until this covering of myelin is completed.

There are two types of brain cells, the actual neurones or nerve cells and the cells that make up the interconnecting structure, the so-called neuroglia cells. The actual neurones or nerve cells have virtually finished their multiplication by about 18 weeks gestation, after which time they grow in size, mature, migrate and form connections. Without these connections the brain would not be able to function any more than, say, the liver. How they connect to the right spot is the subject of very intense scientific study.

How, indeed, do the 100 billion nerve cells connect to the right parts of the brain? What has been found is that to achieve the precision of the adult pattern, neural function is necessary. The brain must be stimulated. The brain must *experience* input for the right connections to be made.

This experiential effect must then have its origins before birth, which has indeed been proven to be the case. The fetus, as well as the child, must be stimulated through the full range of functions such as touch, speech, images and perhaps emotion to develop fully. The necessity for neural activity to complete the development of the brain has many advantages. One of the most interesting is that it is genetically conservative. The alternative, where each connection of each nerve cell is programmed in the genes, would require an extraordinary number of genes, probably billions. We know that the human has only 100,000 genes. It is much more economical for the model of experience to be a major factor in the formation of brain connections.

The first step in understanding the process of experiential learning in the development of the brain has been made in the study of the development of sight or vision. Initially the nerve cells and connections are elaborated in an immature pattern of connections that only grossly approximate the adult patterns. Connections are made to the correct general area in the brain. The incorrect connections are eliminated and the correct ones stimulated through experience, or in the case of vision, the input of light.

In the development of sight or vision, important clues to the role experience plays were found with congenital cataracts, cataracts present at birth. If the condition is not treated promptly, it can lead to blindness in the affected eye. That is, if the cataract is operated on too late, light reaches the back of the eye and is transmitted by the nerve to the brain but would not register, as the part of the brain corresponding to vision perception and transmission would not have adequately developed. It needs the *experience* of vision to complete its development.

The experience is translated to action potential, or microvolts of electricity along the connections. The nerve cells that fire electricity connect together. The front of the eye works like a camera, projecting an upside down picture of the world to the back of the eye. The light is then converted to minute microvoltage electricity and transmitted down the axons of the nerves to the brain. The pattern of connections is so precisely ordered that the image of the outside world is repeated in the brain precisely in the form of electrical impulses. The development of this part of the brain needs practice and experience to get it right!

These remarkable facts have far-reaching implications. Could enriched environments enhance development by actually stimulating brain growth and connections at all levels of function of the brain, from simple reflexes to morality? It certainly puts an emphasis on the importance of prenatal life and experience. Preliminary research that shows such things as enhanced verbal skills and musical ability in children who were exposed to language and music programs in the womb could be explained by the experiential model. Perhaps we should not be carried away, however. The experiential model could just potentiate normal development, or ensure that we reach our genetic potential, not produce a super person.

The most amazing aspect of the formation of connections is what happens if a wrong connection is made. If the error is not too great, the axon can be made to shift its connection; if it is too great, the whole nerve cell, the connection and its cell of origin will die. In fact, half of all our nerve cells will die in the development of the brain in order that the right pattern is made in the end. Degeneration and cell death is a normal part of prenatal development.

With this knowledge of structure of the brain has now come research and knowledge about the function of the brain before birth. How does the fetus move and function? Are there behavioral states in the fetus? How much can the fetus hear, see, taste and learn? How is the personality molded before birth, if at all? What part does psychological trauma and stress have to play in the development of the baby?

By raising these questions we are now entering the controversial area of the development of consciousness. How conscious is a fetus? When does consciousness commence? The fetus is no longer the stranger to us that it was in the past. The fetal human no longer develops unseen but is photographed in utero with the aid of ultrasonography or ultrasound. We can view the moving fetus long before a woman can feel movements or stirrings. Our relations with the fetal human have multiplied. These studies have been nothing short of astounding.

Correlation of the development of the brain and spinal cord and fetal movements is possible. Although the nervous system is still relatively immature, connections between nerve cells of the brain and spinal cord are very rapidly occurring from six to seven weeks. The total complement of actual nerve cells is largely present by 16–18 weeks though many connections still have to be established.

The brain stem is the area of the spinal cord just below the brain. Within it is a richly interconnected nerve cell network called the reticular formation, which has the ability to self-generate an ongoing activity—therefore it can function as an impulse generator. The fetus at eight weeks has started to develop this system and is able to generate spontaneous movements rather than simple reflexes. This corresponds with the first non-reflex activity. The small out-pouching below the brain, called the cerebellum, which is responsible for balance, coordination and fine movements, lags behind and does not finish development until later in the pregnancy or even newborn period.

The earliest recorded electrical brain activity is at seven weeks, corresponding with the first movements. This activity is scant and disorganized, however. The brain waves become increasingly regular after 10 weeks, at the same time as general movements of the fetus begin. These brain waves are seen as relatively discrete bursts of repeated activity in place of an early intermittent pattern.

Development proceeds at a great pace, with the number of connections within the spinal cord increasing seven-fold in the eighth week and four-fold from week 11 to 13. It is known that at seven and a half weeks the mouth region is sensitive to external stimulus. By the age of nine to 10 weeks reflex activity can be initiated by stimulating the palm of the hands, the genital area, the soles of the feet, arm, back and shoulder. The muscle stretch receptors that detect contraction and stretching of the muscles appear at nine weeks and this sensation of movement is fed back into the brain.

The multiplication and migration of the nerve cells of the brain continue for about three months, finishing at 18–19 weeks, after which the first connections appear between the brain and the spinal cord. The connecting fibers pass through a structure just below the brain called the thalamus.

When are these connections made? When do the true connections between the spinal cord and the brain take place? When do we start to develop the sophisticated functions of the human brain? The best answer is a relatively imprecise one, probably a bit past mid-gestation, about 18–22 weeks.

Australian Aboriginal custom dictated that the baby's first kick corresponded to the moment of spirit conception, when the soul or spirit entered the body of the fetus. The mother-to-be marks the spot and rushes off to fetch the elders of the tribe, who then interpret the lie of the land and decide which spirit has entered. It enters, according to the Aboriginal, by "jumping up" either through the mother's toenail, up her vagina or into an open callus on her foot and works its way into the womb, impregnating the fetus with spirit and song.

Early anthropologists reckoned that the Aboriginal did not connect sexual intercourse with pregnancy. This is nonsense, as it was known very well who the father was. The parallel paternity of the spirit is as magical and beautiful as any of the Aboriginal customs.

And the Aboriginals were right. The fetus at 18–20 weeks is finally "connected"—the brain is connected to the spinal cord and the fetus is a person, with a spirit. Surely the baby is influenced then and after by the mother's environment—broadly speaking, her "situation in the landscape".

As far as brain waves are concerned, the first truly patterned brain waves are obtained at about 20 weeks, at about the time that the brain nerve cells start to make very vigorous connections. The first sustained brain waves at 22 weeks and the emergence of two patterns at 30 weeks mark the differences of wakefulness and sleep. Finally, as the normal time of birth nears, alternative waking/active sleep and quiet sleep brain waves make their appearance. The fetus is prepared for its birth.

6

The Importance of Movement Before Birth

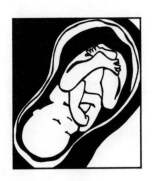

Fetal muscular movements arrive as soon as the muscles develop. By six weeks after conception there are smooth, worm-like movements of the fetal body. By eight weeks there are rapid irregular movements of the whole body, with bending and extending movements of the trunk and with slight movements of the limbs. The position of the baby is not changed by these movements. By nine weeks there are general movements, with the whole body curling up. Isolated arm movements commence at nine and a half weeks and isolated leg movements at about the same time. Rotation of the head commences at 10 weeks and hand/face contact—the beginning of thumb sucking—commences at 10 weeks. Jaw opening and stretching movements commence at approximately 11 weeks and yawning, sucking and swallowing at 12½–13 weeks. By 13–14 weeks there are creeping and climbing movements (symmetrical limb movements).

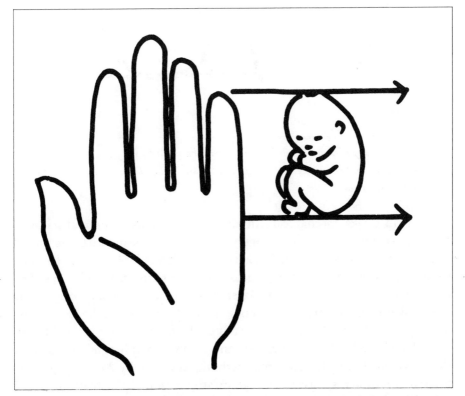

AT 12 WEEKS *the fetus is about 5cm long, or about the size of your little finger, from its head to its bottom. From* Pregnancy and Birth. *New South Wales Department of Health. Used with permission.*

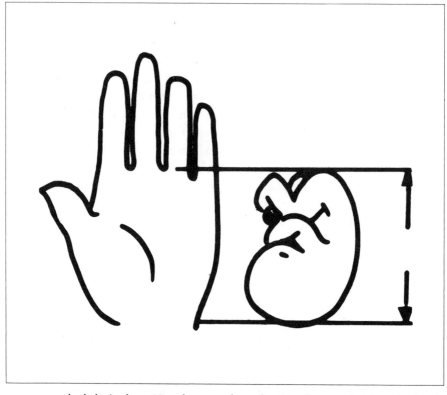

AT 16 WEEKS *the baby is about 10cm long, or about the size of your palm, from its head to its bottom. From* Pregnancy and Birth. *New South Wales Department of Health. Used with permission.*

At 15 weeks, mechanical stimuli on the mother's abdominal wall will produce a startle response. The fingers are actually in the mouth being sucked at this time. At 16 weeks there is good coordination of limb movements. The hands may be clasped together and sometimes both move sideways. The hands explore the uterine and placental surfaces, and when the body is extended, the head is thrust against one side of the womb and the feet against the opposite. By 18–19 weeks the hands of the fetus explore its own body.

By 22 weeks there are sudden and vigorous diaphragm contractions (hiccups) which usually occur in a rhythmic sequence. By 24 weeks there is head rotation and response to mechanical stimulation. Fetal breathing can be very frequent, especially after maternal meals or the administration of glucose. By 26 weeks there is the start of trunk and head rotation responses, and an increase in heart rate in response to sound—the fetus can hear. These latter responses can be inhibited if the stimulus is very loud or is repeated at short intervals. There are bursts of activity.

One of the most interesting facts is that individual movement patterns of the body, which are recognizable at an early fetal age, change very little during the pregnancy. What is remarkable is that there is a similarity between before birth and after birth reflexes and qualities and patterns of movement.

The differences after birth are only in the amount and strength of movement, probably because of the increased influence of gravity after birth and the learning period required for the vestibular or balancing system in the middle ear. Presumably this system was not being used in the womb, where the fetus found a position of comfort in the relatively weightless environment of the swimming pool of the amniotic cavity.

Patterns of activity, sleepfulness and wakefulness have already been established prior to birth. These patterns have been recorded by ultrasound. The sometimes quick, sometimes slow, mostly uncoordinated, but sometimes coordinated, extension and flexion of arms and legs in the newborn are nothing else but a continuation of intrauterine movement. This is seen in observations of babies who are premature. Their movements vary little from intrauterine movements. When approaching their actual birth date, these premature babies do not change their repertoire of movements in a way that would indicate any major reorganization at 40 weeks or true birth age. As far as movements go, therefore, there is no indicator for readiness to be born. Birth is not accompanied by a profound change in nervous reflexes, action or behavior.

Thomas Browne, in 1642, had remarkable insight when he wrote, "Every man is some months older than bethinks him: for we live, move, have a being and are subject to the action of the elements, and the malice of diseases in that other world, the truest microcosm, the womb of our mother".

The baby in the first month or two after birth tends to maintain many of its prenatal characteristics; this is especially true for social interaction, vision, postural control and conscious learning. These apparently limited capacities possibly explain the insecurity and mild dissatisfaction some mothers, especially those who are inexperienced, feel about their infants. This situation changes dramatically about the end of the second month after birth when the number and complexity of movements, actions and behavior enable the infant to cope and communicate with greater efficiency with the outside world. But why this curious delay in development?

Basically, the reason for the delay is not known but seems to have a lot to do with the immaturity of the human baby at birth compared with other animal species and the evolutionary reasons for this. As explained previously, the human baby, it seems, is born a year too early, probably because the head would be too big, if the baby were born later, to pass through the mother's birth canal. The human brain is the biggest in proportion to the body of any animal. The price to pay, it seems, is a very immature newborn baby, needing a lot of care and attention.

7

The Baby's Life Support System

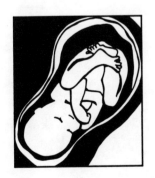

How does the baby sustain its growth and nutrition? In the first couple of weeks when the embryo is a collection of cells, diffusion from the mother's bloodstream is sufficient to nourish the tiny embryo. The embryo soon outgrows such a system and its development requires a larger and more efficient method of obtaining nutrients. A structure forms at the interface of the womb and embryo; this is the placenta or afterbirth. This is the life support system for the embryo/fetus: part mother, part fetus. It is a throwaway organ discarded at birth but essential during pregnancy as it has the functions of a lung, digestive system, kidney, a food store and a source of essential hormones for the growth and maintenance of the fetus.

At the "business" end of the placenta are finger-like structures called villi that penetrate the wall of the uterus. The mother's blood circulates between these villi, bringing the maternal and fetal circulations close together, separated only by a membrane. There is no intermingling of the mother's blood and the baby's blood, and the mother's blood is at a considerably higher pressure than the baby's, which is thought to help the interchange of nutrients, oxygen and carbon dioxide. The welfare of the fetus depends more than any other factor on the adequate bathing of the villi of the placenta by maternal blood. Essential nutrients are now actively transported or pumped to the baby by the placenta. Under-nutrition in the mother, or even starvation, will affect her much more than her baby. The famine in Holland at the end of World War II caused only a small drop in birthweight and there appeared to be no significant long-term effects on the babies after birth.

In a way, the baby is parasitic on the mother, who will suffer nutritionally before her baby will. For example, glucose, the most important sugar for energy, is present in the mother's blood at a higher concentration than in the fetal blood. It therefore passes readily to the fetus. The fetus either uses the glucose to produce energy or stores it in a variety of tissues and organs. The passage of glucose to the fetus is facilitated by a glucose transporter. The placenta is an active organ and as such needs energy—this is also supplied by glucose. No wonder the mother usually has a sweet tooth and an increased appetite as she has to support growth of the fetus and as well provide the power supply for its life support system.

All nutrients have to cross the placenta. Because the concentration of some nutrients is less in the mother than in the blood of the fetus, these nutrients have to be actively transported across the placenta. One example is iodine, which is essential for development of the thyroid gland and the brain.

Similarly, nutrients such as the amino acids that produce protein need to be actively transported, and that active transport needs energy, which is supplied by the glucose needed to "run" the placenta.

The placenta also acts as the "lungs" of the fetus. The lungs have developed, and indeed the fetus is breathing, but as the fetus is not in contact with the air and oxygen of the outside world, the placenta is the organ that absorbs oxygen from the mother's blood and gets rid of the waste carbon dioxide gas from the fetus. Oxygen is taken up more readily by the fetal red blood cells, as the cunning fetus has a special form of haemoglobin—the red substance in the blood cells which carries oxygen—called fetal haemoglobin, which is more efficient than the "adult" haemoglobin in the mother's blood cells in catching and holding on to oxygen. Also, the fetus can function at a lower oxygen level than that of the mother. Clearly, the mother tries to

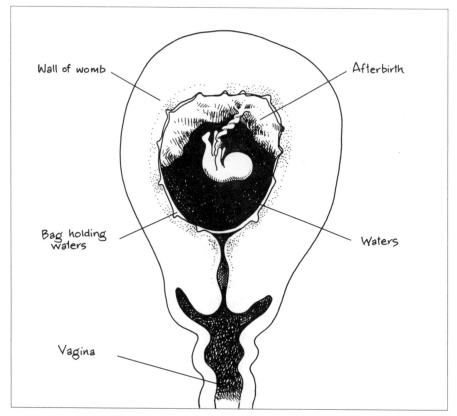

FROM Pregnancy and Birth. *New South Wales Department of Health. Used with permission.*

transport oxygen efficiently to the placenta. If she is anemic herself, however, the fetus can be compromised. If she smokes and increases the amount of carbon dioxide and carbon monoxide in her blood, there is less oxygen to transport, as the carbon monoxide and dioxide bind irreversibly to the mother's haemoglobin. Unfortunately, the fetus cannot store oxygen.

The placenta also acts as a kidney, to enable the fetus to get rid of waste products associated with energy consumption and body building. The fetal kidneys do produce urine, but this is contributed to the bag of water surrounding the baby and to subserve other functions of the kidney, such as maintaining salt and water balance, to exercise the kidney in preparation for an independent existence.

As well, the placenta is a major producer of hormones, which maintain the pregnancy and facilitate the growth of the fetus. Growth-like hormones, thyroid-like hormones and sex hormones are secreted by the placenta. In fact, the ovaries of the pregnant woman can be removed after the first trimester without affecting the pregnancy. The sex hormones progesterone and estrogen are produced in large amounts by the placenta. They are important in maintaining the pregnancy, in the process of birth and in maintaining the increased blood flow to the womb during pregnancy. A fifty-fold increase of blood flow is necessary to maintain fetal growth.

The secretion of a hormone, chorionic gonadotrophin, by the placenta during the first weeks of pregnancy is the basis of all pregnancy tests performed on the urine or blood of the mother. This hormone promotes the production of the sex hormone progesterone from the mother's ovary prior to its production in the placenta. The fetal organ, the placenta, therefore, secretes a hormone that acts on the mother's organ, the ovary. This is an early form of two-way communication.

The placenta eventually covers about one-third of the inner surface of the womb, and is usually positioned at the top of the womb. During the first four months it is larger than the embryo which it feeds and sustains; in the last five months the embryo/fetus grows more rapidly than the placenta. At four months 50 pints of blood flow through the placenta every day. By nine months, just before birth, it is about 600 pints!

The placenta is unique and mysterious. It is the only organ produced from two individuals—the fetus and the mother—the fetal tissue being deeply embedded in the mother's womb. It breaks all the rules—normally foreign tissue is rejected, even that of first-degree family members. The tissues of parent and child are usually non-compatible. But the pregnant state of the mother produces tolerance for the "foreign" tissue of the fetus. This unique ability to override the immune systems of both fetus and mother is essential in maintaining the contact and function of the placenta. Because of the relative lack of immunity which is a necessary result of this, the mother can be prone to serious infection during pregnancy.

There is tantalizing new evidence that the fetus may be able to influence its environment by the production of hormones from its placenta. For instance, the placenta produces the hormones corticotrophin releasing factor (CRH) and adrenocorticotrophic hormone (ACTH). These will act on the mother's hormone system to increase her protein breakdown to provide nutrients for her baby. If the fetus is stressed, these hormones are released and have their action on the mother. The action of ACTH is to release the stress hormone cortisone, to produce a classic response to stress, the flight or fight response. The fetus, although not connected by nerves to the mother, can communicate its distress and needs by hormones produced in its own organ, the placenta! The psychology of the pregnant woman is different and thus these steroid hormones, such as cortisol, can produce mood states such as elation or depression. The fetus, therefore, may be indirectly responsible for this by influencing its mother's hormone levels! And the separation at birth could conceivably produce a "letdown" and may influence post-birth depression in some susceptible women.

Ancient cultures treated the placenta with reverence, according it a ceremonial burial. A mystical or magical notion was attached to the after-birth. In many cultures it was regarded as a double of the child. For nearly 3000 years, up to 300 BC, the ancient Egyptians had a cult of the placenta. A standard representing the royal placenta was carried before the pharaohs of that time. The placenta was referred to as the Bundle of Life, the Life Giver, the Sun, the seat of the eternal soul.

The umbilical cord connects the placenta to the baby. Inside the umbilical cord run two arteries and one vein, and it is the baby's heart that pumps the baby's blood to and from the placenta. As the placenta and umbilical cord have no nerve supply, cutting the cord after delivery is not painful to the child or its mother.

At fertilization we weigh ½ one millionth of an ounce; at birth, on average 7 pounds. In the nine months from conception to birth we increased our weight 2 billion times! Where did all this material that makes up so much of our bulk come from? As a Professor Dubzhensky puts it, the answer, in a word, is groceries. And how do they get to the fetus? By the placenta. We are what our mothers eat.

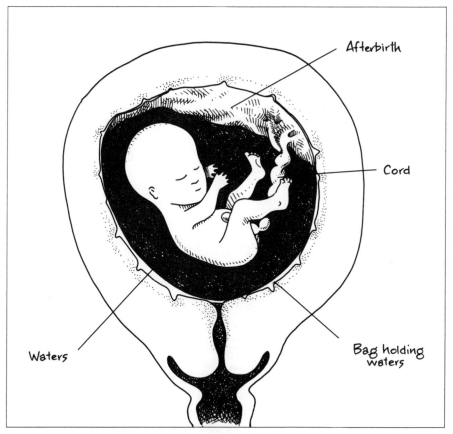

FROM Pregnancy and Birth. *New South Wales Department of Health. Used with permission.*

8

Fetus and Family

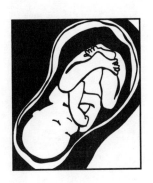

An understanding of life before birth, both in structure and function, is important not only for scientists and anatomists but also for all intelligent adults whose biological responsibilities are to produce and nurture the next generation. With this newfound information we can give to the fetus not only respect for its structure and function, but also for its feelings. We must realize the fetus has a personality. Although its behavior may be rudimentary by our standards, this developing human's life before birth should be given the same consideration and respect as that of an adult.

We may all live to grow old, but we were once a fetus ourselves. As such, we all have been connected with this stage in life. Most of us are able through the renewal of the generations of both our own children and our grandchildren to get some insight into these matters, at least on an emotional level. The human's ability to adapt to adverse circumstances is massive and, although it may not affect our life's course, a greater understanding will make this course more enjoyable, smoother and possibly productive. The sharing of the remarkable experience of life before birth will bring us closer to our parents and our family and to our fellow humans.

The newborn baby and its mother, as Thomas Verny says in his book *The Secret Life of the Unborn Child*, are old and loving acquaintances at birth, who cannot wait to set eyes on each other. Bright-eyed and alert, provided it is not drugged or traumatized, the baby searches for its mother immediately after birth. When the mother speaks, the child often tries to turn its head to her.

Althea Jauch Solter's well-received book *The Aware Baby* has four basic assumptions: that human beings are born knowing basically what they need for optimal physical, emotional and intellectual development; that they are born with potential for both good and bad behavior; that early experiences can have a profound and lasting effect; and, finally, that such knowledge can put people at ease. Dr Solter's book is full of interest and is an excellent approach. However, the frontiers should now be pushed back. They need to go beyond the concept of the aware baby to that of the aware fetus. For the baby in the womb is well equipped to respond. Later in this chapter recent research concerning the ability of the fetus to feel, hear, taste, see and think will be discussed. The fetus *is* aware and responds.

Psychological research indicates the existence of critical periods for development. The critical periods when stimulation does the most good are known as imprinting periods. If babies are not touched and held in the first six months of life, they become apathetic and neurotic. There are hundreds of clinical studies as well as experimental animal work concerning the importance of sensory input. Most are concerned with tactile stimulation and sound contact such as voice. Some have shown a failure of the brain to develop if deprived, as shown in the visual system, especially as demonstrated by the cat model. The visual system within the cat's brain will not complete its development unless exposed to visual experiences—light, dark, movement, patterns and colours. The higher the species in the evolutionary ladder, the greater the effects of stimulus deprivation.

Understanding that life before birth is the beginning of our sensory experience and orientation to the world must make these prenatal experiences critical for normal development. If the fetus does not experience its senses or is deprived of stimulation, its development will be affected. Research in this area is preliminary—most has been done after birth when the baby is accessible—but our thinking should now go back to the time in the womb and appreciate that positive prebirth experiences are critical for our normal psychological development.

HEARING

Research into the ability of the fetus to hear sounds has given enormous insight into prenatal development, personality and learning. From the structural, and probably functional, points of view all parts necessary for hearing in the ear are present at 24 weeks. The baby shows definite responses, mainly in heart rate, to sounds at 24-26 weeks. In a 22 week fetus there is no response, which is possibly due to the absence of nerve connections at this stage.

Sounds are carried to the baby's ear not by air but by bone, liquid and flesh. It had been thought that the fluid that surrounds the baby, the amniotic fluid, fills the ear canal, and in addition to resulting in fluid in the middle ear, would impair hearing in the womb. In the past it was considered that the external sounds would be muffled due to this fluid barrier and obscured by the normal gurgling sounds of the tummy and the rushing sounds of the blood, particularly in the main blood vessels, which are quite close to the womb. These sounds have been measured at a very loud 85 decibels, something like sitting halfway back at a pop concert.

However, in an effort to determine exactly how and what the fetus hears, Drs Armitage, Baldwin and Vince, in the prestigious journal *Science*, looked experimentally at sheep. Inside the amniotic cavity, where the fetal lamb is enclosed in a "bag of water", they sutured hydrophones or underwater microphones next to the ear. The mother's blood vessel sounds could not be heard and the sounds of the mother's gurgling bowel were just discernible. From their research they have indicated that external sounds could be heard fairly clearly, but were dulled by 10–30 decibels. This means that external conversations, particularly of those close up, could often, but not always, be understood, but raised voices were almost always distinct. Even with a 10 decibel loss of hearing, the fetus would still be able to hear a conversation across the room, a door opening, a cart going down the hall, even with the door closed.

Further experiments have confirmed that the mother's voice forms a prominent part of the intrauterine sound environment and that her voice may be louder in the womb than just outside the abdomen! The reason for

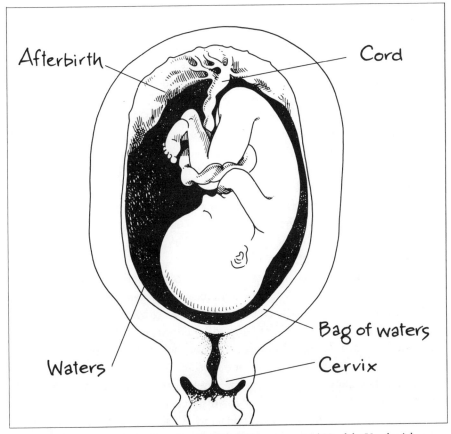

FROM Pregnancy and Birth. *New South Wales Department of Health. Used with permission.*

this is that the sound can be directly transmitted through the mother's body, not just out at the mouth and back in through the abdomen.

The middle ear and its drum and tiny bone chain, although functional weeks before birth, are not necessary for the fetus to hear. Fluids, tissues and bone have good conductive properties and the sounds can reach the inner ear via the body's tissues with negligible loss. There may be no need for the amplification system of the middle ear! Previous recordings taken from pregnant women in the last stages of labor, after rupture of the bag of fluid, do indicate a dramatic cacophony of sounds such as gurgling of the bowel and rushing of the blood.

The Japanese have produced recordings of this intrauterine sound environment for commercial release, marketing them for their ability to soothe the irritable and crying baby. Both parents and nursing sisters have insisted that babies immediately quietened down, listened and slept when the recording was played. Scientific studies showed that as long as the baby was not hungry he/she did stop crying and went to sleep.

Further studies have shown that these recordings were similar to "white noise", which has also been shown to induce sleep in babies. So-called white noise is sound which has tones across the full spectrum of the human ear—low, middle and high tone. Most parents have found that various forms of white sound will soothe their baby. Vacuum cleaners and the noise inside a car travelling at about 30 miles an hour are two examples—who hasn't heard of the baby who will only settle when driven around the block! This sound needs to be quite loud—70 decibels—for it to have an effect and, for induced sleep to occur, the baby must not be hungry. Some white noise emitters have now been marketed to soothe babies. White noise will not suppress intensive stimuli such as hunger so that it will not deprive the baby of a feed. The basic needs still have to be met.

The intrauterine recordings and white noise should not underestimate the importance of the maternal voice. Babies will quieten and listen to their mother's voice, and especially to the mother's voice *and* handling. What the mother needs to know is that her baby will quieten and relax, as long as he or she is not in pain, hungry or uncomfortable when talked to, sung to and handled by her. Handling will provide further tactile stimulation and other sensations. The baby can recognize the smell of its mother as well. After all, they have lived intimately together for nine months!

An article by Anthony Decasper and William P. Fifer in the journal *Science* showed that the newborn baby recognized and had preference for its mother's voice compared with that of another female. The infants in this study lived in a group nursery and their general care and night feedings were handled by a number of female nursery personnel. At most, they had had 12 hours of postnatal contact with their mothers before testing.

This early preference is possibly due to the babies having remembered rhythmicity, intonation, frequency variation and phonetic components of speech. It also suggests that these infants are profoundly influenced by auditory experience before birth. To recognize the mother's voice so soon after birth, the baby must have been listening before birth. The newborn baby responds less well to male voices, including the father's; the lower frequency male voices are possibly masked by the lower frequency background noise in utero. In addition, as already discussed, the mother's voice is transmitted directly from her voice box or larynx to the baby through her body.

When does the recognition of voice or true listening start in the womb? Drs Anthony Decasper and Melenie Spence, again in the journal *Science*, showed that the baby could not only respond to its mother's voice, but could be taught to recognize a particular nursery rhyme and preferred its mother reading it compared with readings by other females or the father. The book used in this unusual experiment was the famous Dr Seuss book *Cat in the Hat*, which has a lot of rhythmicity and rhyming in it. The babies preferred their mothers reading this to the story *The King, the Mice and the Cheese*. Both books were read for five hours in utero.

Studies suggest that newborn babies may find the mother's actual language more attractive than a foreign one, indicating that they have become familiar with the sounds of the language when a fetus. Not only did babies born to French-speaking mothers discriminate between French and Russian when spoken by a bilingual woman, those babies born to mothers who spoke a different language were unable to discriminate between French and Russian at all. They recognized the lilt, inflections and rhythm of the language that they experienced within the womb, in their life before birth.

By 32 weeks, eight weeks before birth, the fetal ear is totally mature, very similar to that of the adult. This is when fetal hearing comes into its own and external sound becomes so important in development. Good friends of my wife's and mine described the following story. The husband was away a lot on business during the pregnancy of their first child. Their favorite songs were those of John Denver, and they had a particular tape which they liked to play together. The mother used to relax every afternoon, put her feet up and to ease the hours and days of separation, would play the tape that both she and her husband enjoyed together. After the birth of her baby she was fascinated to find that her baby immediately quietened, stopped crying and became relaxed when she used to switch on that favorite John Denver tape.

Peter Hepper of the Department of Psychology at Belfast University reported in the prestigious British Medical publication the *Lancet*, the experiences of a group of women who liked the Australian TV soap opera *Neighbours*. They used to relax in the afternoons and early evenings, put their feet up and watch this very popular TV program. There is a nice catchy theme song to *Neighbours*. This group of women noted that after birth their babies stopped crying and became relaxed when the *Neighbours* theme came on the TV. This group of mothers were compared to those mothers who had not watched the program. The babies of the mothers who had not watched the program did not quieten down when the *Neighbours* theme came on.

In response to this letter to the *Lancet*, Mary and Anthony Birch reported a different effect. They reported that during the first stage of labor before the birth of their fourth child, they played several games of backgammon over a few hours, to help pass the time. This game produces a distinctive rattling sound as the dice are thrown onto the board. For about four months after their son was born they were unable to play backgammon without him waking and crying, despite the fact that he would be undisturbed by other much louder household noises. This boy was obviously disturbed by this sound. Perhaps he was reminded of the discomfort of birth!

A friend of mine, who was 30 weeks pregnant, attended a concert with her mother-in-law. The concert was very contemporary in nature, with a lot of percussion and jarring music. At a particularly percussive point, the mother-in-law placed her hand on the mother's abdomen "in case the baby was frightened". There is a great well of custom and knowledge that has been neglected about the care of the unborn baby. The instinct of this woman in her magnificent gesture may be a reflexive response to a deep and hidden knowledge in human culture about life before birth which survives in our modern scientific community.

Dr Robin Panneton has done in-depth research on the effect of music in the womb. He asked pregnant women who were near to term to sing a melody every day for the rest of their pregnancies. Sixty-three infants were tested after birth and were given choices as to whether they listened to the familiar melody or an unfamiliar melody. The infants preferentially selected the familiar melody.

Professor Don Shetler, of the Music Education Department at the University of Rochester in the state of New York, America, has been studying the effect of music during pregnancy on infant development. This research is preliminary, as the babies have yet to grow up and be observed. The fetus is exposed to stereo hi-fidelity sound by placing earphones directly on the mother's abdomen without any clothing or obstructions. The listening period is 5–10 minutes. The immediate responses were not surprising. Stimulative music was responded to by rather sharp, rapid or agitated movement, but with more rolling or soft music, fetal movement was slower.

Of more interest are Professor Shetler's observations after birth. By the age of two, 80 percent of the children will play a toy piano with one finger at a time, whilst unstimulated children will just bang several random keys at once. The stimulated children will pick out different melodies and try them at different places on the piano, and will often sing them as well. Shetler notes a side benefit—the development of highly organized and articulate speech. Although the research is as yet incomplete, Shetler believes that prenatal music may give babies a head start.

The effect of music in the womb may influence a child's whole life. Yehudi Menuhin, the famous violinist, had the violin played to him daily by his mother during her pregnancy. He is convinced that this exposure had a profound influence on his art. Artur Rubinstein, the famous nonagenarian pianist, recounted a similar experience, and Alicia de Larrocha, one of this century's most renowned pianists, revealed to Dudley Moore in an intimate TV interview that her prenatal environment of music from her family, principally her mother who was an accomplished classical pianist, influenced her excellence and her profession.

Thomas Berry tells of a film made by Yehudi Menuhin at the City of London Maternity Hospital in which Menuhin demonstrated that it was possible to contact the newborn via music. The fetus appeared to prefer the flute, because it was a single sound, rather than the music of Beethoven which is much more complex. According to Michelle Clements, fetal preferences include Vivaldi and Mozart, which have a calming effect. The fetus is disturbed not only by Beethoven but also by Brahms.

Studies on animals, particularly birds, have generated the opinion that it may be important for the baby to recognize the mother's voice in order to bond with her. The hearing ability of the baby bird just before hatching appears to be acute. Specific vocalizations of the incubating parent bird may regulate prenatal behavior and hatching time and, in many bird species, it appears that the young recognize their parents by voice, which is crucial for them to receive food, warmth and safety. In crowded nesting sites individual recognition of the parents by the chick is needed immediately after the hatching, otherwise they would be easily lost in the crush. Although the human infant cannot make sounds in utero, it seems that the birds can make sounds in the egg. With ducks, it seems that in addition to visual and other cues, the auditory or hearing identification of the mother by the duckling is something to do with its experience of its own voice.

Perhaps the Bible should have the final word on hearing in utero. Luke 1:44 says, "For behold, When the voice of your greeting came to my ears, the babe in my womb leaped for joy".

TASTING

Taste is present in the human fetus quite early, at least at six months gestation. Experiments on fetal rats found that putting a bitter-tasting fluid into the fluid cavity around the unborn rat resulted in it immediately recognizing this substance after birth, which caused it to switch to another drink. Those who had not had this experience were prepared to put up with the bitter taste in order to get fluid.

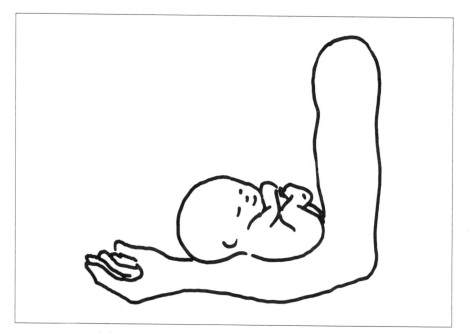

AT 24 WEEKS *your baby is about 21 cm long, or about the length of your elbow to your wrist, from its head to its bottom. From* Pregnancy and Birth. *New South Wales Department of Health. Used with permission.*

Using very refined techniques, another experiment gave rat fetuses a mint solution, which they apparently perceived as pleasant. The fetuses began moving, rotating and making mouthing motions. They were then given a bitter-tasting solution, which made the fetuses stop moving. Two days later, the ones who had been given the bitter-tasting solution after the mint were presented with the mint again and stopped moving just as though they had been given the bitter-tasting solution. Dr William Smotherman, who did these experiments in Oregon State University in 1981, concluded that these rat fetuses were able to learn in late gestation and they could express their learned responses in utero to sensations of taste.

Dr M. Desnoo injected saccharin, an artificial sweetener, into the fluid sac surrounding the human fetus and reported an increased swallowing rate of the fetus. Presumably it liked the sugar taste! Dr A. W. Liley of Auckland, New Zealand, investigating swallowing by human fetuses, noted a marked decrease in swallowing after an injection of a noxious-tasting substance used for x-ray studies. The fetuses were aged 34–39 weeks. Immature taste buds are recognized on the tongue at seven weeks and are mature by 12 weeks gestation. It is likely that the fetus uses its taste receptors to monitor its own environment.

SEEING

The fetus can see from six months onwards. Premature infants can open and close their eyes from 25 weeks gestation; the fetus in the womb almost certainly does the same. Responses of the fetus in the womb to bright light that is shone through the abdomen include changes in the heart rate and turning away. However, in normal conditions, the interference of the surrounding tissues and the now cloudy surrounding fluid, the boring view and the lack of adequate illumination, probably prevent the fetus from obtaining a worthwhile image.

At birth, the baby can see well at short distances, but doesn't know what he or she is looking at! Certainly, fetal eye movements are obvious from 16–18 weeks. Initial movement is in the form of a transient single movement from mid-position to the outer, lower eye margin, followed by a return to the original position. Then prolonged single sideways deviation follows, giving way in the third trimester to complex sequences of brisk, jerky deviations, and later in the third trimester to repetitive movements.

Increasing phases of eye inactivity are noted later in the third trimester, implying inhibition, which occurs during deep sleep. The scanning movements continue to develop, occurring, in particular, during certain sleep states called rapid eye movement sleep. Rapid eye movements during sleep are also seen in the infant and adult. These movements are probably not for seeing but to exercise and develop the muscles that cause the movements. Unless they are exercised and the eyes are moved, muscles will become wasted and scarred.

Many advances in the last 10 years have indicated that the fetus and young babies have much more perception and experience than was ever imagined. Research on very young babies gave added insight into the capabilities of the fetus, or at least the very mature fetus of seven to nine months, when experience really does count. Scientists have learned a great deal about very young babies. We now know that they can tell objects apart by their shape, size and colour. They know that these objects go on existing when they are hidden and they can also take in whether they are solid or not. When they look at and listen to someone talking, very young babies can tell whether that person's lip movements are the appropriate ones for the speech that they are hearing. But is this just proof of perceptual ability rather than reasoning?

Further evidence for thinking ability includes demonstrations that these very young babies can recognize the number of a set of objects and can tell when there has been a change in number, and they can do this for small numbers irrespective of changes in the special arrangement of the set. They can tell whether the number of drumbeats that is played to them coincides with the number of objects in a visual display that is shown to them at the same time. This appears to go beyond simple perception.

Dr Karen Wynn, in the prestigious journal *Nature*, has recently shown that not only do young babies take in information about the number of objects before them, they are also able to work out the results of addition and subtraction! Dr Wynn showed that alert, well babies looked significantly longer at incorrect displays of both addition and subtraction. The objects were little Mickey Mouse dolls, and one, two or three objects were used, with the babies being shown an addition or removal of dolls, and expected to respond to true or false answers.

The sceptical may wish to look at the original work before being convinced, but it is accepted by *Nature* that Wynn's evidence is cast iron. The main question is whether the baby can understand math or whether the ability to do such tasks is innate and unnecessary to learn. Of course how this ability correlates with later mathematical ability and even whether such activities enhance later ability in that specific area also needs to be asked. Intriguing and radical, but on present knowledge plausible. The implications for education and assessment are obvious.

Why do the senses mature so early in the pregnancy? Experience before birth is an important part of normal human development. The fetus must feel, hear, see and taste to be born an integrated and prepared person, to finally meet its mother, its family and the world. When trying to determine which abilities or responses are innate to the baby and what it learns from experiences, it is shortsighted to consider only those events which take place after birth. The fetal experience cannot be ignored.

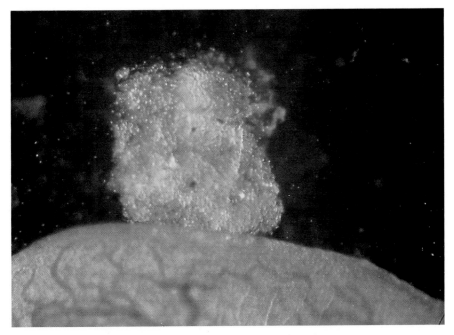

The moment of ovulation. The egg is clearly visible emerging from the ovary.
Coloured photos: courtesy of PETIT FORMAT/NESTLE ©

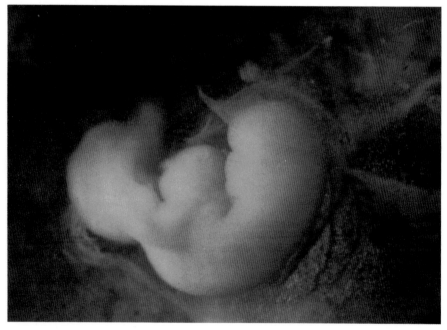

Human embryo at four weeks.

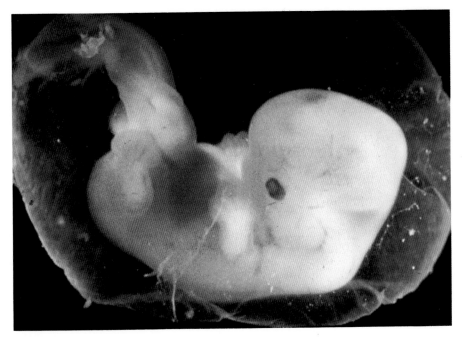

Embryo at six weeks.

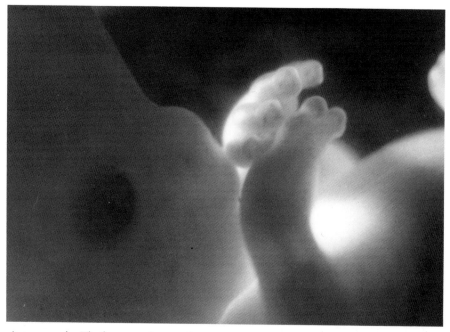

At two months. The fingers are just starting to separate.

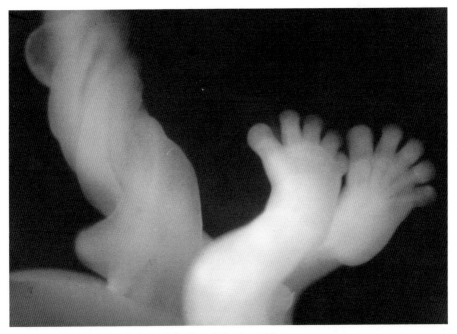

Fetus at two months, with the umbilical cord clearly visible.

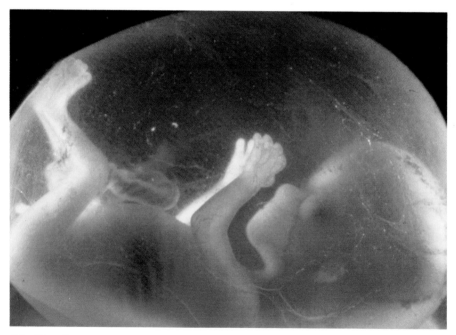

14–15 weeks.

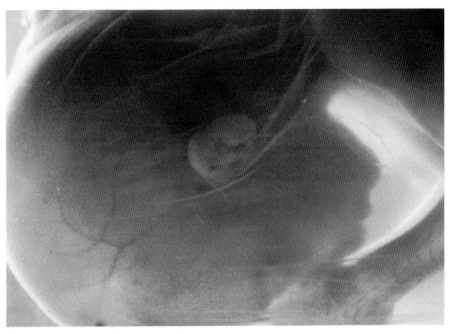

Fetus in the early second trimester.

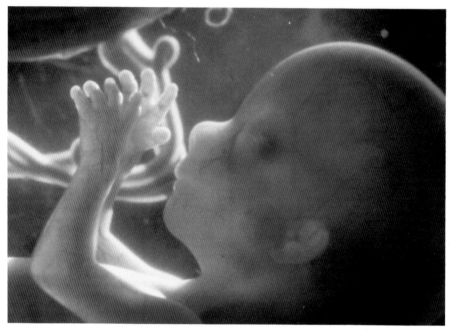

Fetus in the late second trimester.

9

The Importance of Environment Before Birth

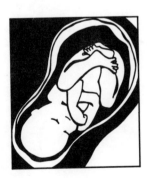

Considerable research has been focused on what things within the environment of the fetus and the maternal, or outside, environment can affect the fetus's behavior and, perhaps, its personality. In the pre-scientific era, complications of pregnancy, labor, birth defects and psychological development in the child were widely attributed to various supernatural causes, maternal impressions and unnatural sexual activity. Indeed, as already indicated, in a lot of primitive societies prenatal advice consisted of methods for protecting, amongst other things, the psychological well-being of the pregnant woman and her fetus. The pregnant woman was often subject to extensive taboos that included her diet, activity, social relations and sexual contact. Certain psychological experiences were to be cultivated or avoided, in the hope of affecting the health or psychological characteristics of the baby, as well as promoting a good labor and plentiful breast milk. Maternal impressions were thought to be very important in the formation of birth defects and monstrosities. For example, the term "hare lip", used to describe clefts of the lip, was thought to be due to a hare or rabbit crossing the path of the pregnant woman. The hare has a natural cleft of the upper lip.

The theory that maternal impressions influence the development of the fetus was very strong in medieval and Victorian times and survives to the present day in many third world countries. This theory describes the viewing of an abnormality or certain feelings as a cause of a birth defect or problem in development, although Hippocrates, the ancient Greek philosopher and physician, refused to accept the maternal impression hypothesis. This theory of maternal impressions is described in all continents and races. Ancient literature abounds with such fantastic theories; for instance, descriptions of babies with the face of a frog occasioned by the mother holding a frog in the hand just before conception.

The elephant man, a grossly deformed Londoner, was exhibited and studied late last century. A film has been made of his experiences starring the well-known actor John Hurt. It is an extremely evocative commentary of a man's feelings when trapped in a severely deformed body. The elephant man ascribed his peculiarity to the fact that his mother was knocked down by a circus elephant during the pregnancy.

The original Siamese twins, who were joined at the chest and exhibited in circuses throughout the United States and Europe in the late 19th century, were banned from entering France because it was thought that fertile and pregnant women viewing them might have similar malformations.

There is endless variety of recorded customs, rituals, foods and habits in all social groups which are thought to improve the health and prospects of the unborn and an equal number of taboo activities, emotions and foods that may harm the baby in the womb. Amongst Mexican peasants an expectant mother must not tie an animal, since her fetus may be strangled by the umbilical cord. The Tongan mother will not wear a girdle or necklace around her neck for similar reasons. Amongst the Yukaghan, a peasant tribe in Asia Minor, no one is allowed to walk or ride around a house where a pregnant women lives since that may cause the umbilical cord to wrap around the neck of the fetus and kill it.

Food rituals are very important in these ancient societies. For instance, in Aboriginal tribes in Australia they forbid a pregnant woman to eat porcupine lest the child be humpbacked. Among some New Guinea tribes a pregnant woman may not eat a bandicoot or else she will die of hard labor, nor may she eat a frog or the child will be born too suddenly (will jump out!), nor the eel lest the child be born too soon (slip out). Some of the Maori tribes of New Zealand used to believe that failure to satisfy a pregnant woman's fancy for certain foods may result in birthmarks, monstrosities or even death of the child. In many of these ancient tribal customs the man is involved as well.

Hippocrates is said to have saved the day for a white princess who gave birth to a black baby by attributing the unusual occurrence to the presence in her room of a picture of a Negro. In ancient Greece a physician called Soranus (AD 98–138) affirmed a belief in the influence of the pregnant woman on the offspring. He gave an account of how the ruler of Cyprus, who was considered to be very ugly, succeeded in fathering beautiful children by encouraging his wife to look at beautiful statues.

Some of the stories have more than a touch of the ridiculous. In Surrey, south of London, in November 1726 it was recorded that a woman by the name of Mary Taft, after being startled by a rabbit in the fields near her home, was said to have given birth, after an appropriate interval, to seventeen rabbits. King George the First, apparently intrigued by this incident, decided to investigate because of the excitement and intensity of the story. The King's investigator, his personal physician St Andre, confirmed the story and recommended that the mother (and himself) be given a royal pardon and income. King George sought a second opinion from another investigator, who had no difficulty in exposing the event as an enormous hoax. Needless to say, St Andre did not get his pardon.

The theories of maternal influence and its effect on the body have left their marks in our language. Birthmarks, in particular, were thought to be due to maternal thoughts or experiences. The German word for birthmark is *muttermal*, literally mother's mark (*mutter* = mother, *mal* = mark, sign). In Danish it is also *modermaerke* (*moder* = mother, *maerke* = mark, sign); in French it is *envie*, literally envy, wish or longing; and in Italian it is again *voglia*—wish, whim or longing. Ashley Montagu, in his book *Prenatal Influences*, relates a story from his childhood that in London in 1916, during a zeppelin raid, his mother's cousin gave birth to a child with a zeppelin mark on its cheek. The stress of the air raid on the mother was thought to have influenced the defect.

The literature of the 19th century expressed the continuing belief in the importance of maternal impressions. Charles Dickens's Sarah Gamp probably expressed the beliefs of her period when she spoke of a man "marked with a mad bull in Wellington boots upon his left arm, on account of his precious mother having been horrified by one...". In the book *Tristram Shandy*, Tristram's father attributed his son's lifelong "simpleness" to the fact that his wife had asked him at a highly emotional and most inappropriate moment in their marital life whether he had remembered to wind the clock. It was possibly to emphasize his feelings about the unfortunate "paternal impression" that Walter Shandy changed his son's name from Trismegistus, "the most propitious", to Tristram, "the most unlucky".

When it was proved that the fetus has no actual nerve or blood connections with the mother, the reaction in the scientific community was to infer that the fetus was isolated in the womb, away from all external influences and only controlled by genetic influences. All aspects, including abnormalities, were thought to be caused by the genes. The placental barrier was thought to protect the fetus from any influences. This was a shift to the other extreme, negating any influences on fetal development. By observing growth, movements and even facial expression of the baby at regular intervals through the use of ultrasound images taken throughout the pregnancy, researchers have been able to show definite effects on the fetus from maternal stress.

An Italian study by Drs Ianniruberto and Tajani looked at 2000 pregnancies. The fetal movements were hyperactive in cases of acute maternal emotional stress. The movements were more numerous, disordered and vigorous. In some cases of very intense maternal stress, fetal movements were inhibited for some time, from two to 48 hours. In all these eight cases, the episode was followed by complete recovery.

Drs Ianniruberto and Tajani, having completed this research, had an opportunity to make a very interesting observation. An earthquake in

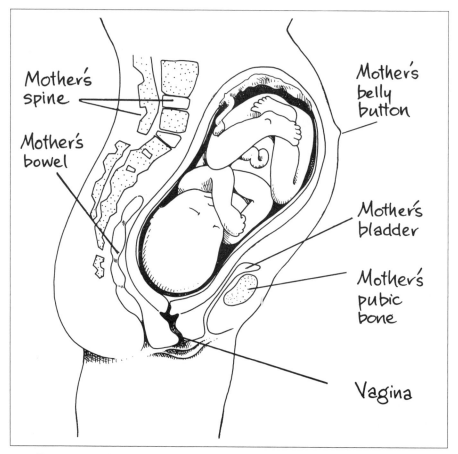

Mother's spine

Mother's bowel

Mother's belly button

Mother's bladder

Mother's pubic bone

Vagina

FROM Pregnancy and Birth. *New South Wales Department of Health. Used with permission.*

southern Italy caused several tremors at the maternity hospital of Terlizzi on 23 November 1980. They examined with ultrasonography 28 panic-stricken pregnant women, from 18–36 weeks gestation, who had suffered no physical trauma. All the fetuses showed intensive hyperkinesia, or hyperactivity, which lasted from two to eight hours. In 20 cases this was followed by a period of reduced mobility and activity lasting from 24–72 hours, while the remaining eight fetuses recovered immediately.

Other abnormalities were shown in these 2000 pregnancies. One 14 week pregnancy was complicated by the presence of numerous large benign tumors of the womb, called fibroids, poking into the womb. The baby's head was imprisoned in a restricted cavity and it fought to be free. The legs repeatedly showed a sort of peddling motion until the fetus succeeded in getting its head out and changing its position.

In a twin pregnancy, they observed a set of identical twins who fought a boxing match with repeated rounds of a few minutes each! One of them started by hitting its twin with its hand and the other would hit back. Rest periods of a few minutes separated the "rounds". The twins were not separated in different sacs.

They also observed a case of a mother who had an electric shock of 220 volts from an iron at 18 weeks gestation. Her baby sat immobile in the womb, did not respond to mechanical stimulation and had a very fast heartbeat. The immobility lasted for a period of 48 hours, but on the third day normal movements were again present. The baby was born apparently normal.

Correlation of individual fetal movement patterns by ultrasound observation before birth and the patterns after birth in the same baby still has to be performed. It has been demonstrated that maternal stress during pregnancy, particularly emotional stress, may affect the baby's behavior after birth, in particular by irritability, crying and loose stools, which may persist for months after birth.

Psychoanalysts have had a field day with the prenatal period. Sigmund Freud was dubious about actual recollection of memories from the prenatal period, though he recognized the importance of fantasies in dreams related to the so-called womb experience. Before entering and originating psychoanalysis, Freud was a Viennese neurologist or nerve and brain specialist. Neurology followed the traditional biological opinion that the child was not able to experience or feel until memory was available—at the second or third year—and that personality development was delayed until then. Freud himself wrote that the womb was "free from stimuli".

Dr Otto Rank felt that the entire process of psychoanalysis involved a reliving of the prenatal experience. Rank wrote a book called the *Trauma of Birth* in 1924. He felt that the satisfaction and security of life in the womb constitute a blissful state which is rudely destroyed by the experience of birth. The individual spends its life, according to Rank, trying to return to the paradise and blissful environment of the womb—"every pleasure has as its final aim the reestablishment of the intrauterine primal bliss". Freud, on the other hand, did not believe that birth is experienced as severe shock, but rather that it produced physical and psychic helplessness. The need for love is created, according to Freud, because of this helplessness. Both Rank and Freud felt that the anxiety of birth was important—the first anxiety.

One cannot but have sympathy for these early psychoanalytic attempts at establishing theories of behavior. But the concept that the fetus is stuporous, asleep or "blissful" and only becomes aware at birth is quite out of date—all the reactions present at birth can be demonstrated before birth. Patterns of activity, movement and the ability to use the senses are not changed by the birth process. There is no change in the maturity or function of the brain at birth.

Indeed one psychologist, Arthur Janov, observed in his book, *Imprints—The Lifelong Effects of the Birth Experience*, published in 1983, that "not only is the fetus affected by what the mother takes into her system—it is equally affected by the state of that system—is that pregnant mother easy going, relaxed and calm, or is she chronically tense, depressed or agitated? Is her life situation quiet and stable or is she encountering crisis after crisis?..." Despite the title Janov selected for his book, he willingly concedes the prebirth experience is of great importance.

Not all psychiatrists agree that the process of birth is a shocking experience. A baby who has had a good birth, without any lack of oxygen and interference at full term, will be physically exhausted, but is unlikely to be psychologically a "wreck". The exquisite beauty and progression of the birth and the extent of the baby's development or preparation for the event is so impressive that to take the view that the changeover from pre- to postnatal life could involve an ordeal as severe as dying is probably wrong. Psychiatrists are now exploring areas of prenatal development, looking at the movement pattern, influences of pregnancy, such as the mood of the mother, as well as physical factors, in their attempts to determine the final psychological state of the baby and, later, the person.

Dr R. Laing, a famous psychotherapist, has urged a stance of openness to the possibility of genuine experience before birth. Intrauterine memories have become a generally accepted interest of psychoanalytic theory. There is no doubt that such theories or studies are very much in an "embryonic" state of scientific proof.

It is tantalizing to think that we may have unconscious memories about life in the womb. We were all a fetus once and, as such, an adaptable, sensitive, receptive person before birth. Most people can't remember to the age of three or four with much accuracy at all. Is remembering within the womb a little farfetched, particularly if, as has been shown, a majority of the fetus's life and the life of the newborn is spent sleeping and eating? The brainwave picture confirms that whilst asleep, we can move and sense, but probably not remember an experience as conscious, except as a dream.

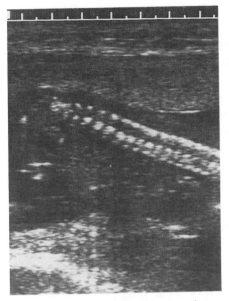

ULTRASOUND OF *the spine. Courtesy of Dr Debbie Wass, Sydney.*

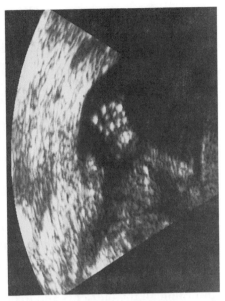

FETAL FOOT *bones. Ultrasound courtesy of Dr Debbie Wass, Sydney.*

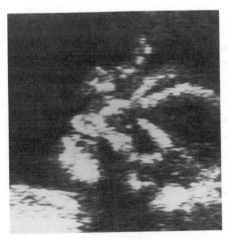

FETAL FACE. *Note lens in eye; tongue; hand next to face. Ultrasound courtesy of Dr Debbie Wass, Sydney.*

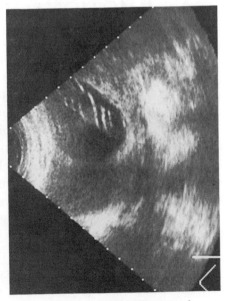

UMBILICAL CORD, *with 3 curling vessels— 2 arteries and one vein. Ultrasound courtesy of Dr Debbie Wass, Sydney.*

It is important to appreciate that fetal behavior is not a trivial aspect of prenatal life.

A variety of substances have been found by ultrasound studies to affect movement and possibly behavior of the baby by decreasing movement and breathing. These substances include alcohol, cigarettes and sedative medications. Although it is not my wish to diminish caution over exposure to various substances, it is important to view the fetus as an active agent in its own development, and this should be seen as a cause for optimism and reassurance. In other words, the fetus can adapt its behavior and its chemistry without any harm necessarily resulting in the final outcome. The fetus's ability to respond adaptively to potentially hazardous events promotes well-being. Many of the excretory or detoxifying actions of the baby get "switched on" after birth, but if the fetus is exposed before birth, the chemical reactions that promote metabolism and detoxification have been shown to be already switched on at birth: the fetus can adapt its body mechanisms and react before birth. It is not helpless and passive like a piece of blotting paper, absorbing all the nutrients and toxic factors of the mother into its system.

An Emotional Life Before Birth

From the preceding facts, the sensory inputs to the fetus before birth, its responses and learning capacities, provide the tantalizing concept that the fetus has an emotional life before birth, that can be adaptive and contribute positively and negatively to development.

Dr Antony J. Ferreira, a psychologist of San Jose, California, reviewed the importance of a positive psychic prenatal environment in his book, *Prenatal Environment*. To be pregnant is to be committed, says Ferreira. This commitment may not be entirely desired. Pregnancy often comes as a surprise, and it has been suggested that the development of the fetus may be disturbed if the reaction is a negative or adverse one. If a pregnancy is not wanted, what outlets are there for the pregnant woman's negativity toward the pregnancy and the child she bears? Guilt, anxiety, depression and fear are found to be the result. As such, *both* the mother *and* the unborn child would suffer and the conflict could display itself in a total organism reaction, both as physical and psychological sickness. Many studies have shown that miscarriage, high blood pressure, prematurity and various birth complications are more common if the pregnancy is destabilized by the mother's (or the father's) ambivalent feelings to the baby, other negative feelings, excessive anxiety, exhaustion and so on.

The study of abnormality has always given insight into normal human processes, both psychic and physical. The study of the influence of adverse factors on the unborn child has enabled insight into the factors that influence the prenatal environment. Drs Sontag and Wallace, in 1934, were the first to show a direct relationship between maternal emotions, fatigue and food on the patterns of fetal activity. Dr Sontag's observations were the first real attempts to look at fetal emotions in a scientific way. The most interesting points, inevitably, were his various anecdotes, which threw light on this subject.

A young woman carrying her first baby, which he had been studying weekly in terms of activity and heart rate level, took refuge in Dr Sontag's institute building one evening because her husband had just suffered a psychotic breakdown and was threatening to kill her. She complained that the kicking of her fetus was so violent as to be painful. A recording of the activity level showed it to be 10 times the normal. Another of Dr Sontag's anecdotes concerned a woman who lost her husband in an automobile accident. Again the activity and frequency of movement of the fetus increased by a factor of ten.

At birth, however, the children of mothers exposed to extremes of emotion showed no birth defect (a fact that was first observed by Dr John Hunter of London in 1782). They were, however, irritable, hyperactive, tended to have frequent stools and marked feeding problems.

In Melbourne, in 1956, Dr Elisabeth Turner noted a relationship between emotional stress during pregnancy and a general tendency to excessive crying, irritability, sleeplessness, vomiting and loose stools in the baby. In 1962 Dr Ferreira, in a comparison of problem babies to normal babies, found that the mothers had revealed a significantly increased risk of having extreme attitudes, such as fear of having the baby and rejection of the pregnancy. Even as early as the 16th century, Leonardo da Vinci stated succinctly that, "one will, one supreme decree, one fear that the mother has, or any other mental pain, has more power over the child than over the mother". This clearly also applies to the mature fetus.

If one lives close to a disturbed person, one runs the risk of becoming deviant oneself. Such as when a partner in marriage adopts the deviant behavior of the spouse for instance, psychiatrists call this phenomenon *folie à deux*. In the case of the mother and child, it is arguable whether the influence is hormonal, that is, the mother's stress hormones crossing to the baby, or psychic, the close proximity of a stressed mother affecting the stress response of the baby, or, as some have suggested, as a consequence of the abuse of cigarettes, alcohol or other drugs taken because of the stressful events. In any event, the unborn baby is encompassed by the emotional currents of the mother.

Consider how sensitive we all are to the emotions and feelings of those around us. We experience positive feelings of love and support, but also negative emotions of fear, anger, resentment and envy. The mother is the encompassing environment, the baby's entire world. The experience in the womb will probably not be consciously recognized later, yet the emotions from these experiences can be as important as post-birth experiences in setting the emotional atmosphere in which a person lives and how a person may look at life.

The baby, before and after birth, does not forget, even if these memories are confined to the subconscious. Acceptance of the fetus as a living being influenced by such factors is central to understanding life before *and* after birth. As a living being, the fetus is adaptable, so there is no reason to think that negative influences could not be compensated for or treated during the pregnancy or after the person is born. It seems obvious that during the last weeks of pregnancy it is important for the mother to develop positive attitudes and to ensure physical and mental tranquillity.

Most women seem to sense the importance of the last weeks, prompted by their anticipation of the birth and the physical necessity for rest. For it is in these last weeks that the fetus is particularly awake and responsive to its environment. The serenity of the woman in her last weeks of pregnancy, her meditative state and placidity can be readily observed and are probably familiar to women who have had their own child and have been through this experience. Many naturally talk or sing to their babies at this time.

Patterns of behavior and development can, of course, be inherent in the baby and not necessarily induced by the events of pregnancy. The sister of a colleague of mine noticed that her baby was particularly active—in fact, the ultrasound at 16 weeks, before the movements were felt, showed that her baby just "wouldn't keep still". She had a problem-free and stress-free pregnancy and a boy was born normally.

During the first year of life he appeared to need little sleep and was restless and irritable. At the age of four years he is still the same: normal in IQ and behavior, but in perpetual motion, continuing the innate restlessness that he showed at four months gestation. This is his own spontaneous activity, the pattern for which was probably determined at the time of fertilization and conception. Perhaps he came from a long line of active persons. We have all known people, perhaps whole families, like this.

The wife of another acquaintance had twins—non-identical—whose progress in the womb was followed by ultrasound. They nicknamed the horizontal one Horrie and the vertical one Vert. Vert had a threatened miscarriage caused by some bleeding under his placenta—he came out the anxious one, whilst Horrie was placid. By six to nine months, however, both Vert and Horrie were somewhat the same emotionally. Here may be an example of reaction and adaptation with the healing effect of time and growth. The continuum of emotional development extends well before birth.

Dr Alexandra Pointelli, a psychotherapist from Milan, Italy, has initiated some fascinating research on personality and behavior before birth. She has extended infant observation to prenatal life. Infant observation is a well-known psychoanalytic technique whereby the family psyche is investigated through observation of a baby.

Dr Pointelli has observed prenatal personality with the use of ultrasound. She observed non-identical twins, a boy and a girl, whose mother was positive and interested in their development. The little boy (Luke) seemed much more active than his sister (Alicia). He kept turning and kicking and changing positions and stretching his legs against the wall of the womb. From time to time he would interrupt his activity and seemed to turn his attention towards his sister. He reached out with his hands and touched her face gently through the dividing membrane. When she responded by turning her face towards him, he engaged with her for a while in a gentle, stroking, cheek-to-cheek motion.

Dr Pointelli's nickname for Luke and Alicia were the "kind twins". Alicia seemed the more passive of the two. Most of the time she seemed asleep, or else would move only her head and her hands almost imperceptibly. She responded each time to Luke's stimulation, only to plunge back into her state of passivity and sleep. At birth, Luke came out first, skinny and bony, but lively and alert. Alicia, who was born last, was calm and contented, just like in the womb!

At one year of age, when they could walk and were beginning to talk, they took great delight in playing with each other. Their favorite game was hiding behind a curtain and using it as a kind of dividing membrane. Luke would put forward his hand through the curtain and Alicia would reach out with her hand and their mutual stroking began, accompanied by gurgles and smiles.

Personal relationships can develop before birth. Some mothers are convinced that their active, alert, interested children are born early, and that the introverted are born later. Certainly some babies make sure they are born.

A patient of mine was convinced her premature, but otherwise normal child "decided" to be born six weeks early. She had moved 4000 bricks the day before and the stress and exhaustion had probably resulted in her baby initiating labor earlier than normal.

If the development of the baby can be impaired from various influences, including maternal emotions, it may also be improved through prenatal care and the influence of positive emotions. There is a lot of discussion and many books that focus on ways to enrich and facilitate educational, cognitive and motor development of children after birth, and there is enormous energy being put into things such as baby gym, card flashing and various teaching exercises. Prospective parents should now consider enriching their baby's development before birth. Our current understanding of the aware baby in the womb reinforces the often overlooked truth that development begins at conception not birth. Understanding of life before birth can help to embrace this view.

10

When Do
We Become
a Person?

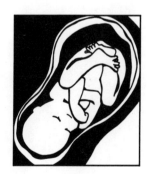

A couple of decades ago, the notion that a fetus possessed a personality would have been laughed at. The pre-Victorian ideas of the fetus still held sway. There is now no reason why unborn or fetal humans should be treated differently from born humans. Nothing important occurs with the development or function of the brain at birth except that the fetus is exposed to the cold air of the world. Concepts and science have moved rapidly.

It is now accepted that the 24 week fetus, though immature, has a personality, can learn and is well advanced in its physical and brain development. How far back can we go? What is the earliest stage at which the fetus would be considered a person, rather than a potential person? What constitutes a person, in the moral and, these days, the legal sense?

Carol A. Tauer, a philosopher who has taken a great interest in this subject, has written a brilliant essay in which she expresses her belief that the elements that link fetal life to the life of a person are the potential to be a person, the presence of brain activity, some sort of psychology and the capacity for sentience or consciousness. None of these factors alone appeared sufficient to Dr Tauer to attribute "personhood" to a human fetus, but some combination of these factors is important.

The focus is the development of the brain—the movements, responses and patterns of the fetus reflect this. Up to about five weeks after conception, the human fetus and its "brain" are very similar in development to that of animals but after that point the massive and unique development of the human brain diverges.

The answer to the question of personhood is a serious one and should not just be fought out on points of logic or debate. The abortion debate and the questions of experimentation on human embryos have exercised the legal and religious minds of our communities and have given rise to considerable acrimonious argument. Scientific and medical knowledge can now be used to put the debate to more stringent criteria, as it is the welfare of the unborn child and the protection of its rights which are our main concern. Legislation has taken abortion out of the back alleys and into the hands of medical professionals in partnership with the mother and her family and this is where it belongs. These involved persons will now have to respond to current research and knowledge.

At the beginning we are one fertilized cell with genes that give us our potential and which will guide our development and life. Scientifically, the fertilized egg is a receptacle for the genes, viability and individuality being determined by groups of cells, all interreacting. Dr Tauer advances the argument that although the genes provide biological continuity, this sort of continuity lacks moral relevance. All these genes are present in each cell in our bodies; we each have billions of cells—surely *each* cell has no moral status. The integration of the whole is achieved through brain functioning and experience, *this* has a moral relevance, more relevance than the genetic pattern in a single cell or a collection of cells.

Dr John M. Goldenring has joined the argument contending that the "at conception theory", which says that a human being exists at the moment of fertilization, may find itself in difficulty if recent scientific predictions become true. As every single human cell contains the full genetic information of any other cell, but expresses it differently, it may become possible to finally clone a single human cell to differentiate into a complete human being. Will we then say that every cell of the human body, say, a skin cell, is a human being?

Also consider the placenta or afterbirth. It is composed entirely of fetal tissue. Each of its cells contains all the genetic codes. If cloning were possible, we could be created from a cell of the afterbirth. Although a vital life support system, it is not considered to be alive and a person, no more than the early egg and cell masses of the fetus should be considered a person.

The potential to be a person is not enough to be invoked as a ground for respect, care or caution. If the fetus is to be respected, cared for and given a moral basis, then it is scientific, medical and social research and not just what the public opinion will accept which should finally bring about our actions on what constitutes personhood.

What are the facts? When does the spinal cord communicate with the processing and thinking part of the brain, the cerebral cortex, where the grey and white matter resides? It is only when the vital connection between the spinal cord processing center, or the brain stem, and the brain itself is made at 22–23 weeks that feelings of the senses such as warmth, light, sound and pain have any real moral (or conscious) meaning and form part of experience. The spinal cord can then communicate with the true brain and vice versa, both responding to movement, feeling and position and presumably, albeit unconsciously, able to have memory which will influence the person for the rest of its life.

On 23 January 1973 the US Supreme Court announced that in the absence of a consensus as to when human life begins it would not speculate on the matter. There is international pressure now to come to a decision spurred by the public's perceived need to control research on in vitro fertilization. In our struggle to reach a consensus we need measured arguments based on solid foundations. We will never prove when the fetus is no longer a potential person and has become real and "conscious". There will be a changing opinion on personhood, and it seems that it can only be determined through applying the results of scientific research. It seems to me that personhood occurs around 20 weeks when the brain cortex is "connected". Some scientists take the beginning of personhood to be when the first spontaneous patterned movements and brain waves occur, at eight to nine weeks.

From your reading, you are now aware that quite early the fetus, though tiny, is not just a clump of inert cells. You are also aware that an unwanted fetus can be emotionally abused before as well as after birth, and this may irrevocably change the life of both the mother and infant. Forcing a reluctant mother-to-be to carry a child may thus be self-defeating. The same argument may be applied to the situation where a child has a severe, handicapping birth defect, particularly when that deficit includes a massive insult to the brain. Ultimately, the woman, hopefully with the support of her spouse, needs to make her own decision. It is indeed a decision not made lightly by most women.

Termination of a pregnancy has complications and side effects both physical and psychological about which a woman needs to be informed. The later the procedure is performed in pregnancy, the greater the medical and psychological risks. Exchanging a pregnancy for a lifetime of guilt and depression is hardly satisfactory. In any event, termination of a malformed or unwanted pregnancy, particularly in the light of recent developments, is a crude approach to the problem of prevention. Clearly, the idea is to detect abnormality at the very early stages or even before conception in the ovum and the sperm.

Remarkable new techniques may make much of the ethical and emotional turmoil about abortion for serious genetic conditions obsolete. At the early four to eight cell stage all the cells in the "ball" that makes up the embryo are pluripotent, can develop into any organ or tissue. Now that it is possible to remove one cell from the test tube fertilized embryo at the four to eight cell stage, the DNA can be extracted and the amount of specific genes amplified to show if those genes are changed or mutated or absent, which would cause a severe genetic disease.

One example is cystic fibrosis, a severe, life-threatening disease of childhood, whose genetic basis was accurately localized a few years ago. At the Royal Postgraduate Medical School in London, England, a team from Britain and from Baylor University in Texas processed one cell from the several embryos produced by in vitro fertilization (IVF) using the eggs and sperm of a couple at risk of having a child with cystic fibrosis. The embryo which was unaffected was implanted. The embryos which were found to be affected with the disease were not implanted back into the mother. A normal baby has now been born. This is an exciting advance in the prevention of genetic disease.

In the *Journal of Medical Ethics,* Dr John Goldenring has made contributions to the argument surrounding personhood. Goldenring takes a radical view, maintaining that attitudes need to be changed. Compare the fetus to an 80-year-old on a respirator in an intensive care unit, says Goldenring. If this person has a functioning brain, even if he or she is unconscious, there is no doubt on the doctors' or community's part that the patient is living; there has been a lot of medical and legal effort in defining brain death.

The fetus is inside the most advanced intensive care unit ever designed, the mother's uterus, and is being ventilated by the most complex extracorporeal respirator or heart-lung machine ever known, the placenta, but our attitude has been to consider its development and brain function to start only at birth. There is no mystery to the process of birth. Disconnecting the 80-year-old adult intensive care patient from the respirator is considered to be a decision that should always involve a team of professionals and the relatives. Disconnecting our fetus should be given the same considerations—whether the person is in utero or ex utero, whether the person will die in the next minute, nine weeks or 90 years, should not necessarily hinder our attitudes to its life. It is not considered that our 80-year-old unconscious patient in the intensive care unit need think or feel to have his or her life confirmed; neither, then, should the fetus, Dr Goldenring argues. The brain forms and starts to function at eight weeks—the first brain waves and movements. Should the life of a human be considered to have begun once this point is reached?

It would be my contention that personhood and sentience or consciousness determines when a human life begins, as this separates us from the animals. The form and function of the first weeks of development are shared by most mammals at least. Development of the unique human form, and in particular, development of the brain and its functions separates us from the animals. Potentiality—that is, the potential for personhood and sentience—is an argument and needs to be taken into account. Respect and care for the potential or actual sentient person should be the foundation of all arguments about when conscious life begins.

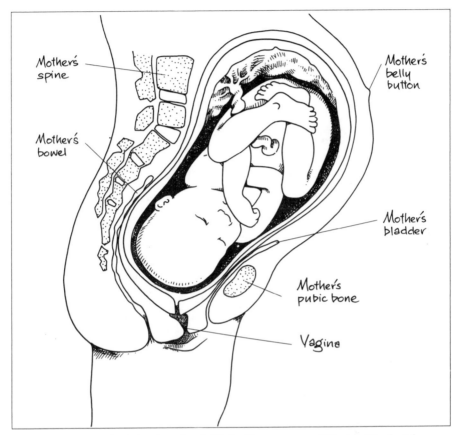

Mother's spine

Mother's bowel

Mother's belly button

Mother's bladder

Mother's pubic bone

Vagina

FROM Pregnancy and Birth. *New South Wales Department of Health. Used with permission.*

11

Birth — A Dramatic Event on Life's Journey

To every thing there is a season, and a time to every
purpose under heaven: A time to be born, and a time to die.
Ecclesiastes 3,5.1

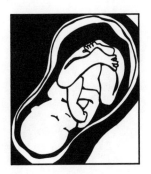

Birth is a complex process that involves not only contraction of the muscles of the womb and relaxation of the cervix or the opening of the womb, but also relaxation of ligaments of the pelvis in order that the fetus can pass (or squeeze) through. The manner of passage of the human fetus from inside the womb to the outside world is not very different to that of most animals, despite the enormous range of sizes and degrees of maturation of the newborn and the structure of the mothers.

Recent research has indicated that it is the fetus that determines the onset of labor, not the mother, and that birth is a maturational event in the fetus, probably no different from later maturational events such as weaning and puberty. The first clues came from abnormalities of the fetal pituitary gland. The pituitary gland is a major controller of hormone production. It is situated at the base of the brain and has connections with the hypothalamus of the brain. The hypothalamus is situated under the frontal cerebral hemispheres.

It was noted in both humans and animals that defects of the pituitary gland, which can occur when the brain is malformed, have resulted in prolonged pregnancies. Experiments in sheep, in which the fetal pituitary was removed early in pregnancy, led to the pregnancy being prolonged. Professor Monty Liggins then went on and removed the fetal adrenal glands: this also caused prolongation of pregnancy.

The pituitary produces the hormone ACTH or adrenocortical hormone which controls the production of cortisone from the adrenal gland. The adrenal gland is situated just on top of the kidneys. The production of ACTH is regulated by corticotrophin-releasing hormone, CRH, which is produced in the hypothalamus, the part of the brain that is connected to the pituitary. Professor Liggins stimulated the adrenal glands of sheep fetuses by giving them *extra* ACTH—they were delivered early or prematurely. Recent sheep experiments have used radio frequency waves to ablate or destroy the part of the hypothalamus of the fetus that produces CRH. This resulted in prolonged pregnancy. So it is the fetal brain, the hypothalamus, which signals the onset of production of extra cortisone and therefore labor.

Throughout pregnancy, the activity of the muscle of the womb is influenced by both inhibitory influences that stop it contracting, and by facilitating influences that make it contract. A sort of balance exists: some promote and some inhibit contraction. Sex hormones, particularly progesterone, produced in the placenta, interact with the appropriately titled hormone relaxin to stop the uterus from contracting during pregnancy. Relaxin is produced in the ovary.

Other sex hormones, particularly estrogen, stimulate the womb. Production of cortisone acts to produce more estrogen from progesterone. Cortisone is stimulated to be released from the adrenal gland by ACTH produced in the pituitary gland, which in turn is released by CRH from the hypothalamus. Cortisone promotes the synthesis and release of substances in the uterus called prostaglandins, which act on the womb muscle to cause contractions, thus overcoming the influence of relaxin.

These prostaglandins are many and various. Prostaglandin E plays a major role in ripening the cervix and in the initiation of labor, while prostaglandin F2 facilitates the normal progress of labor. There are other types of prostaglandins, but they have nothing to do with labor.

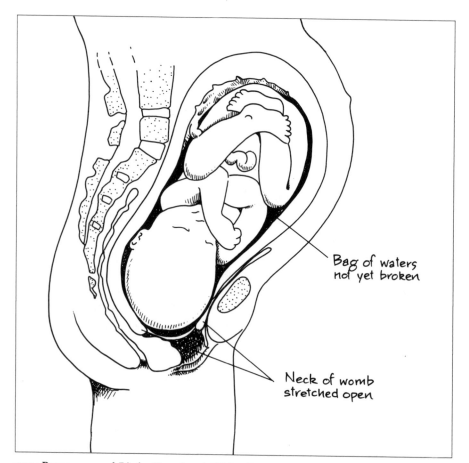

FROM Pregnancy and Birth. *New South Wales Department of Health. Used with permission.*

The fetus communicates with the womb during the pregnancy and tells the womb when to start contracting! Once the womb starts contracting, it tends to become independent of the circulatory hormones and proceeds with its task. The first signs of the change in balance of hormones that initiate labor is in the tightening and small contractions felt by the pregnant woman in the two to three weeks before labor commences. The mother is mostly an interested bystander in determining the onset of labor.

Or perhaps it is more realistic to say that the mother and her fetus act together to decide. The predilection of mares to foal in the hours of darkness, of rats to deliver in daylight hours, and of rabbits to withhold birth when they are observed are well established facts. The alpaca, a camel-like animal farmed in the South American Andes, and the source of that wonderful wool, will only deliver in sunshine, except on cold days. The human has a slight tendency to favor the night. The mother can have some influence on the progression but not the initiation of the birth process.

Relaxin prepares the cervix, the opening of the womb, for birth by causing it to become less firm and to increase its ability to distend. Prior to labor, the cervix remains tightly closed, retaining the baby in the womb. Relaxin also makes the ligaments of the pelvis distensible and stretchable. Little is known, then, of the reasons for premature labor. Perhaps in some premature births there is premature maturation or precocious development of some kind, resulting in a premature initiation of the birth event. Incidentally the hormone relaxin is also produced in the male testis, where it appears to have an effect on increasing the motility of the sperm and enhancing fertilization of the ovum or egg.

Birth, as already indicated, has been treated rather cruelly by psychologists, child developmentalists and indeed obstetricians. Birth is pictured as a fall from paradise, a type of death-like experience, the first experience of anxiety and, indeed, as being able to mold our whole psychological development. It is also often depicted as a painful and traumatic experience for the baby. Some obstetricians have even tried to change the environment of birth so that the baby will not "suffer". Underwater birth is a radical approach, in which the baby is delivered underwater and slowly brought to the surface so as to have a gentle entrance to the world. But does the baby suffer in the normal process of birth?

During birth the baby's head is twisted and abuts onto the pelvis and sacrum or tailbone. The baby itself moves through 90° and sometimes 180° during labor. The fluid that surrounds the baby acts as a buffer and lubricant. There is not much room in there. The baby is not floating in a warm, blissful and protected pool of fluid in the later stages of pregnancy, but is folded and flexed and molded to fit the shape of the womb and the birth canal of the mother. It can't be very comfortable; if there is too little fluid, or anything that may reduce the space of the womb such as fibroid tumors in the uterus, a very small pelvis or a multiple pregnancy, the baby will be molded even more. Wry neck at birth, some forms of twisted foot, dislocated hips and facial molding can result. Up to 5 percent of babies may have significant deformation at birth, which mostly resolves spontaneously once the roomy outsides are attained. Some, however, need special treatment, especially those with dislocated hips, as the hips may not become relocated by themselves.

So it can't be comfortable, the birth process. Yes, it is a radical change and stress, but is it a "death-like experience", a "hell" that is never forgotten, a trauma that is forever with us until our dying day? These extremes are unlikely.

Consider the baby's passage through the birth canal. It can be very painful to the mother. The mother's body is being stretched, whilst the baby's body is being squeezed. Stretching hurts more than squeezing, particularly stretching of tubes or cavities which contain muscle such as the uterus. The actual pressures on the baby during birth are comparable to the pressures on an adult's body while he or she lies in bed. The force of uterine contractions reaches no more than an average of one pound per square inch, the maximum being two to five pounds/square inch (one to three kilograms) on the head whilst the cervix or entrance to the womb is being dilated or is enlarging. Contractions and labor can have a caressing and massaging effect—even, according to some, a sexually arousing effect on both the fetus and the mother.

So it is hurting and stressing the mother much more than it is hurting and stressing the baby. Efforts to make labor more comfortable and relaxing for the mother are extremely important, as this will make the birth more enjoyable, smoother, quicker and will result in less need for obstetric interference. Squatting positions and birthing chairs, soft lights, relaxation and visualization techniques, support persons or relatives are all more important than attempts to stop trauma to the baby. The baby should not, however, be ignored at birth and ways in which the baby can be communicated with during labor are dealt with in the last chapter.

One popular fallacy in our society is the belief that women of other races and different cultures have a much easier confinement. Especially those women in primitive societies are reputed to be able to have a much shorter period of labor, to be subject to less pain and be able to resume their daily tasks immediately following a birth. Our fantasy of the Asian woman squatting in the rice paddy to have her child, then continuing with the harvest with the newborn baby suckling at the breast is extremely common.

Anthropologists who have studied birth in primitive societies categorically deny that a confinement is any easier for women in a primitive society. Few of the primitive societies of the world allow a birth to take place without some experienced person in attendance, usually a midwife. However, some observers have persistently indicated that women in some societies have an easier birth. In this respect, it is important to take into account the cultural background.

One's society and culture will determine how the woman in labor is supposed to behave. In the villages of northern Japan, for example, birth is a highly secret affair. A woman in childbirth, living as she does in the typical flimsy dwelling, with paper screen partitions and in close proximity to her neighbors, avoids, at all costs, crying out during her labor or delivery, or letting her discomfort be known in any way. Social disapproval and considerable embarrassment await the woman who violates these mores. In such an example an observer might easily note that delivery for the Japanese peasant woman was exceptionally easy.

A baby who has difficulties at birth is not likely to develop problems as a result of brain damage from lack of oxygen at the time. The fetus and the newborn are supremely adapted to low oxygen, as the environment of the womb provides an oxygen environment about one-quarter of that available to the newborn baby. The fetus thrives in this atmosphere as the oxygen-carrying substance in the fetal red cells, haemoglobin, has a much greater carrying capacity for oxygen at a lower pressure than the older child and adult.

The huge majority of so-called brain-damaged babies have no trouble at birth. The beloved Apgar birth scoring system (after Dr Virginia Apgar), in which the infant is given a score out of 10 for heartbeat, color, breathing and activity, has not been shown to correlate with cerebral palsy, mental retardation, hyperactivity or epilepsy. Those that have a low score are often responding badly to the stress of birth due to a pre-existing brain problem—that is, the child is not damaged at birth, but its actual brain development before birth has been affected, causing the problem, which manifests during birth as distress and after birth as problems with adaptation and development.

Despite the greater number of premature babies now surviving and being treated, and the improved standards of obstetric care, the incidence of cerebral palsy, for instance, has remained remarkably stable over the last 30 years. Seventy percent of all babies with cerebral palsy are full term and not premature. Of those babies that had a stormy birth process, only about 1–4 percent develop cerebral palsy or are spastic. A large proportion of this 1–4 percent are subsequently found to have a predisposing brain developmental problem to account for their troubles. Even with the tiny premature baby, those that go on to get cerebral palsy are notable for having had a normal, uncomplicated delivery, and do not have more breathing troubles, jaundice or lack of oxygen than the premature babies who are normal. The brain is not damaged but abnormal in its development.

"Brain damage" as a term has distressed generations of parents and has been used through the courts to blame the obstetrician for conditions that he or she did not cause or aggravate. This emotive term, the period of life involved and the current community attitudes have all combined to cause this current opinion. Epilepsy, mental retardation and hyperactivity have also not been correlated significantly to a compromised birth. The fetus may well be scared, anxious and stressed during labor and birth, but, with only a few exceptions, seems able to make a complete recovery from the process of birth with no long-term physical or psychological effects. Indeed, the normal adaptation to the outside world is more likely to require effort and to place stress on the baby in order to proceed smoothly. The birth-stressed baby will manifest exhaustion and sleep excessively for a couple of days, but will then recover and wake up.

A quote from the 19th century author Oliver Wendell Holmes is an apt description of the process of birth:

So the stout fetus, kicking and alive;
Leaps from the Fundus, for his final dive,
Tired of the prison where his legs were curled,
He pants, like Rassalas, for a wider world;
No more to him their wanted joys afford,
The fringed placenta, and the knotted cord.

12

Helping Baby During Pregnancy

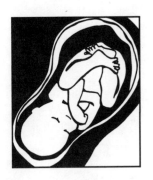

It should be evident from reading this book that the baby in the womb, particularly after five months or 20 weeks of development, is able to react to its environment. Its responses become more marked and sophisticated as the weeks of pregnancy go by. With this dramatic surge in knowledge comes the desire of parents and families and their professional helpers to use this knowledge to enhance and facilitate their baby's development before birth. This is a logical extension of well-accepted techniques and practices to potentiate development of the infant and young child after the birth.

Anything from music to flash cards, baby gym to baby swim are used successfully to enhance the development of our youngsters. How can families start such a program during the actual pregnancy?

A holistic approach should be used. This is a term applied to the care and nurture of our bodies as a whole, not just the body, but the mind and the spirit as well. The holistic approach indicates that if we ignore any of these areas we lack a complete or whole approach to our health.

The mother should take care of her body; her health is crucial to the health of her baby. There are dozens of advice manuals about diet and exercise during pregnancy. Avoidance of excess caffeine, nicotine and alcohol are obvious, as is the need for a balanced and nutritious diet.

To provide care for the mind, the expectant mother may explore visualization techniques, affirmations, art and dream therapy. Meditation in its many forms is a very effective way to quieten the mind. There are a huge variety of groups to help people connect with these techniques.

The importance of the spirit should not be ignored or underestimated. There is great value to be gained from initiating, promoting and enhancing our spirituality.

Which of the available techniques is right is a matter of choice for the individual mother and her family. No one method or group has all the answers for everyone. It is interesting to observe the relaxed and natural way in which many expectant mothers can undertake relaxation, meditation and contemplation in the second half of pregnancy. Whether this is a natural reflexive adaptation, or hormonal, or whether it is just a social phenomenon that is passed from generation to generation is worthy of exploration, as professionals should facilitate these reactions to the advantage of the baby.

As already emphasized, the tranquillity of the mother will bring much benefit to the unborn child. In traditional American Indian culture, pregnancy was a community affair: the whole tribal and community effort was to support the woman in a healthy pregnancy, rather than the responsibility of being pregnant being borne by her alone, keeping up with a million other things at the same time. As has already been mentioned, the ancient oriental customs of the Chinese and Japanese included special prenatal clinics purely to ensure the tranquillity of the mother, which was believed to benefit her unborn child.

Our modern society, with its stripped nuclear family, and the myth of the superwoman, mitigates against tranquillity during pregnancy. The pregnant woman, often without relatives to help, is expected to keep house, care for older children and have a job as well: to be, as the well-known author Sheila Kitzinger says, "Cook, courtesan, intellectual comrade, sympathetic mother, erotic mistress, tender lover and social hostess".

Society admires the woman who works right up to the birth and goes back to work soon afterwards—and who is surprised and negative when the infant is irritable and unsettled. Cultures which have organized themselves to provide maximum support of the pregnant woman are often scorned as ignorant and unsophisticated.

Communicating with the unborn baby in a structured way that is based on what is known about the baby's responses is a logical way to approach this issue, so that not only is the baby being communicated with and stimulated, but positive emotions, thoughts and experiences are also conveyed to the mother and her family. The full acceptance of the fetus as a member of the family before birth will move the bonding time to the prebirth period. The father, children and even other relatives should form positive expectations as a result of such an approach. This is *prebirth bonding*. An awareness of the advanced nature of prenatal development and the consciousness of the fetus, particularly in the second half of pregnancy, as described in the previous chapters, cannot help but make this a logical next step.

BONDING BEFORE BIRTH

The bond should not start at birth. American psychotherapist Eve Bowen, in her book, *Prebirth Bonding*, gives a 10-step program:

Step 1—Rest and relaxation: You cannot be good to your baby (fetus) unless you are good to yourself. Set aside a quiet time to be together with your partner and baby—it need only be 5–10 minutes. Do nothing active, just be together, a quality quiet time.

Step 2—Enjoy the baby: Try to verbalize your feelings, your plans, your hopes and dreams with your partner. Plan the baby's room, furniture and clothes. Think of names.

Step 3—Make contact with the baby: Do this through touch and play, as introduced by Dr Rene Van der Carr's Prenatal University, which is discussed in more detail later.

Step 4—Talk to your baby: At first this is through mental or visualization techniques. Begin the love and nurturing and try to transfer this to your baby, even very early in the pregnancy when the baby is not aware of its surroundings. This is still an important time. Contact is later made through music, speech and touch.

After five months the baby can hear quite well, and responds to music and speech. Playing a favorite tune whilst relaxing and bonding will be an enjoyable experience for the fetus. This tune can be played during labor and after birth to relax and calm the baby. As the fetus and baby will recognize the mother's voice, talking to the fetus is not just for the mother's internal satisfaction and tranquillity but is an actual bonding process. The baby after birth is totally familiar with its caretaker.

According to Eve Bowen, "... talking to your baby is hardly a waste of time. Not talking to your baby would be the waste".

Step 5—Share your whole life: Increase the amount of time you and your partner spend with the (fetus) baby, especially after five to six months, and integrate it into your life.

Step 6—Vocalization: Standard vocalization techniques are important. Use the imagined "movie screen" or "blackboard" techniques. Imagine you are in a movie together and vocalize and visualize the plot. Likewise, imagine you are a teacher writing on a blackboard for your student, your baby.

Step 7—Education: Attend antenatal classes, buy tapes and videos, read books, become an expert.

Step 8—Preparation: Prepare for the birth. Continue rest periods, vocalization, music, talking and touching.

Step 9—Materialization: Put plans into action. Perhaps prepare a written agreement for you, your partner, your support person, the nurses and your doctor to sign. Be assertive. There is a birth day to celebrate. Make your preparation secure.

Step 10—Actualization: This is it! Enjoy the experience of your baby's birth day. Throw out your misconceptions. Trust your intuition.

Note: To do a visualization as mentioned in Step 4, a written plan is important. A friend of mine wrote his two children a letter, just after the pregnancy was confirmed. In it he related his philosophy: that he did not mind whether the child was boy or girl, that the child was really wanted, even in the first trimester, that he had many desires and dreams for his child, but that he hoped that they would be their own person. This is a beautiful idea, formally establishing the relationship and communicating at such an early stage—at least seven months before birth. Perhaps both parents should write a combined letter.

PLAYING WITH YOUR UNBORN CHILD

It can now be seen that actual play with the unborn child is possible. One game for the last trimester consists of the mother gently pushing with her fingers on one side of the abdomen and then the other. If the baby is awake and facing the fingers, the fetus will often push back with its limbs. A thrilling experience of contact with the unborn child for any parent! With this empathy comes early bonding and acceptance of the fetus as a person. This technique is certainly worth a try.

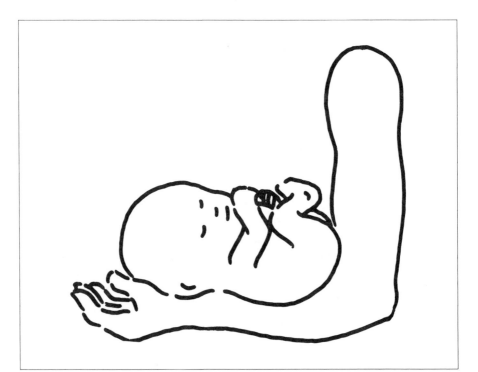

AT 32 WEEKS *your baby is about 25cm long, or about the length from your elbow to the base of your fingers, from its head to its bottom. From* Pregnancy and Birth. New South Wales Department of Health. *Used with permission.*

It is important to be gentle and to be aware of the child's position at the time. Be patient, as the baby is asleep most of the time, even in the womb. Recognition of those times of the day when the baby is quietly active in the womb, in a calm, playful mode and not hungry—such as after the mother has had a recent meal—is important in the application of this technique. The absence of a response can be due to many reasons such as position, not being firm enough, the baby being asleep or not being receptive. Regular sessions of prenatal baby stimulation and contact, at a relaxed time for the mother and family, are also important in obtaining a response to her finger play.

Undoubtedly the pioneer in the integrated approach of play and bonding is Dr Rene Van der Carr of the Prenatal University, based on the west coast of the United States. He now has many imitators. Dr Van der Carr indicates that 5–10 minutes of stimulation twice a day, or preferably two to three times a day, initiated after a meal when the mother is tranquil and the fetus is "awake", is all that is necessary.

Mothers sign up when they are pregnant and then, starting at five months, the mother and other members of the family, especially the father, talk, pat, rub and squeeze the baby in a structured way. Music, vibration and light are also used. The purpose is to alert the baby (fetus) to the fact that certain sounds, motion, vibration and even light can have some meaning, and to initiate communication and bonding with the fetus not just by the mother but also by the father and brothers and sisters.

THE KICK GAME

Dr Van der Carr's program starts with the kick game, which teaches the baby to respond to patting and rubbing, as well as voice and music. The game focuses on that part of the abdomen where the fetus naturally kicks. The baby is spoken to and asked to kick in that spot again; the abdomen is rubbed and patted in response to the kicks. It's a great thrill for parents to realize when the fetus actually responds by kicking. The talk, according to Dr Van der Carr, should be "baby" talk... "Mummy (or Daddy) is talking to you, please kick Mummy again, do it once more". It is the association of sounds and hand pressure that the fetus responds to and learns to communicate with. Of course, it cannot understand literally what is said, but this does not prevent communication. Complete attention must be given to the fetus during this time.

PROGRESSIVE COMMUNICATION AND BONDING TO THE FETUS

From the seventh month onwards, Dr Van der Carr advises that the mother find the position of the head, back and bottom of her fetus. The purpose of this is to facilitate communication, so that vocalization should be directed to the face, and tactile approaches should be made to the body, particularly the arms and legs.

She should lie on her back but be turned slightly so that her weight is on the left side. The mother should speak at a high volume, but not quite shout. The father should moisten his cheek with water for better sound conduction and place this cheek on the abdomen, near the baby's head. Simple words accompanied by the appropriate actions are used to communicate and teach the fetus to respond to these pleasurable sensations. The words are pat, rub, stroke, squeeze, shake and tap and are spoken to the accompaniment of the appropriate action. Pat and rub are repeated—"pat, pat, pat", "rub, rub, rub". Stroke is applied to the fetus's back—"stroke, stroke, stroke". The squeeze exercise is done by applying gentle but firm pressure to both sides of the abdomen—"squeeze, squeeze, squeeze". Shaking is done by placing the palm of the hand on one side of the abdomen and pushing in and out in a rhythmic movement—"shake, shake, shake". Tapping is done with one finger against the baby's head—"tap, tap, tap".

MUSIC FOR BONDING

Dr Van der Carr's program includes gentle music, which should be a favorite tune of the parents, played gently near the abdomen using a cassette recorder. The baby should be involved in activities and talked to—"Mummy is climbing the stairs", "Mummy is sitting and relaxing" and so on. The family should be "introduced" and should try to communicate with the fetus. "This is Grandma, how's my lovely baby?"—the same sort of talk that goes on after birth. This is an extension before birth, when the baby's senses are already active and responsive.

Dr Van der Carr suggests that the same piece of music should be played at the end of each exercise program, and be played intermittently during labor and at delivery, in order to calm and reassure the fetus that its family is near.

The Prenatal University program emphasizes the bonding and positive expectancy in communicating with the baby rather than the making of super intellects. The commitment of the father and the extended family in the pregnancy is reaffirmed and the sharing in the commitment to the baby's development has beneficial effects for the mother, enhancing the spiritual approach she takes during pregnancy, and clearly benefits the fetus and child. "Talk to your baby", says Dr Van der Carr.

A Prospect For A Positive World

Of course, Dr Van der Carr has introduced in a formal way what certain groups have been doing for centuries: communicating with the unborn. In the past it has been lullabies, prayers and so on. And although one may remain sceptical about whether super babies may be produced this way, it is the positive effects on personality and family development that result from such a program that appear obvious in the light of the newfound knowledge about the sensitivity of the prenatal environment.

The baby's acceptance and bonding can now commence well before the baby is born and Dr Van der Carr claims that the positive acceptance of the fetus as a family member before birth has the potential to reduce abusive behavior to the young infant and to establish a positive set of behaviors toward the baby before birth. This seems a reasonable result of his programs.

The Role of the Father

Fathers are important in their own right not just as a genitor or support for his partner but in his own male way. Ying and Yang, animas and animus, the complementary effects of men as well as women must be recognized for good bonding and communication.

In the recent past, Western man was treated only as the genitor and external economic provider and was excluded from all other roles; not so in ancient and primitive societies. In some societies the father is given almost as important a role as the mother. For instance, with Brazilian Indians the father joins in the food restrictions. With the Malay Indians the father is not to cut his hair. In other societies the father should not fall, otherwise he may induce miscarriage. Amongst the Masai tribe of Africa the husband must not laugh at old or crippled persons whilst his wife is pregnant lest the baby be crippled too. The Hopi Indians hold that the prospective father must not lasso or tie an animal, otherwise the child will become entangled with the umbilical cord. The Hopi must also avoid the taking of life. Similarly the Arunta tribe males of central Australia are prohibited from hunting big game.

A common and fascinating paternal participation practice is the custom of couvade. This requires the father at or before the child's birth to behave as if it were he, not his wife, who suffered the pains of labor. This incredible concept was, and still is, remarkably widespread. Diodorus, a Greek of the 1st century, described its practice among the Corsicans; Marco Polo in the 13th century describes it in Chinese Turkistan. In Guiana, in South America, the father actually takes to his bed with grunts and groans, a behavior also common in the Bantu tribes of South Africa. Dr Anthony Ferreira is tempted to say that the practice of couvade and other paternal acts may express an intuitive awareness among primitive peoples and the ancients that, at least in the ways he can affect the mother, the father does have the potential to affect the child before birth.

A delightful practice, described with relish by Dr Van der Carr, is one where the father places his mouth on the mother's abdomen and communicates in this way. This is good for the parents' sensual relationship, as the father often feels he is left out during pregnancy. A full sexual relationship often wanes as the pregnancy proceeds and the mother becomes preoccupied with herself and her baby. Participation of the father will help to overcome his natural jealousy. Some psychologists feel that this jealousy, coupled with loneliness, frustration and tension and the sense of being unloved, often commences with his (the father's) experience with a younger brother or sister when he was displaced in the family by their birth.

As the pregnancy proceeds, the man may feel increasingly shut out. He may try to become intimately involved and be quite fussy in relation to the pregnancy. If scorned, he may withdraw into a man's world. Therefore, the participation of the man in the pregnancy and the development of the baby before birth is a very important aspect of pregnancy.

Sex during pregnancy has often been treated as a taboo subject. Some cultures and religions ban it. Some scientific studies appear to suggest that sexual intercourse can induce labor and prematurity. Many friends, when they know of my interest in the prenatal environment, ask me directly or indirectly about the safety of sex during pregnancy. In the chapter on birth I talked about the hormone relaxin and its role in the birth process. One of the effects of this hormone, which is produced throughout pregnancy, is to relax or stop the womb from contracting. In the male, relaxin is produced in the prostate gland and it is therefore present in the ejaculate. Could intercourse, therefore, act to *stop* labor commencing?

Nonetheless, care with sexual intercourse during pregnancy is prudent. Certainly in the last trimester, the shape of the mother necessitates the couple adopting new positions. Violent orgasm and deep penetration become less possible. Fantasies about the baby "observing" the parents in their intimacy, being scared by the sexual act are just that—figments of fertile imaginations! What would be more positive for the pregnancy and the baby than the parents endorsing their love by a, perhaps, gentler sexual encounter?

The fetus does respond to sexual intercourse, especially orgasm. After all, it is aware, particularly of the mother's activity. There have been studies of the fetal reaction when parents have sexual intercourse in the last half of the pregnancy, at a time of heightened sensory input. Couples have monitored themselves and their fetus and have shown that, as expected, orgasm caused excessive fetal activity with both slowing and quickening of the heart rate after both female and male orgasms. One can only speculate on the emotions of the fetus. The "primal scene" may be quite frightening to experience, although without anxiety and with love the emotion of the fetus may be positive. Who knows?

The important thing is to recognize that the fetus does experience and respond to its surroundings. Care and bonding occurs before birth, and the parents should be consciously aware that the fetus is aware too, and is only too willing to respond to all experiences, and to learn from them. To appreciate this often requires effort and that our minds be cleared of the prejudices of our own upbringing and the dogma and "science" of the past. Parents, especially the mother, need to be true to their own observations and need to be supported with respect to these feelings. The womb, our first environment, need not necessarily be a safe place. The parents' task begins before birth.

More recently, modern man has been included in the birth process and invited into the delivery room to provide his wife with support. He should now be invited to participate in the pregnancy and be considered an integral part of the process of the life before birth of a baby. And, of course, children and even relatives can participate as well. In stimulating and playing with the baby in the womb, the communicators should, however, have cognizance of the sleeping and waking patterns of the fetus and not attempt to overstimulate the baby, who needs its rest a lot more than we do!

Claims as to the superior development of the infants stimulated and bonded during pregnancy have included enhanced physical milestones such as tooth eruption and the development of highly organized and articulate speech. Such claims are preliminary but tantalizing.

MAINTAINING A HEALTHY LIFESTYLE

A healthy lifestyle is, of course, the goal of any woman who is concerned about the growth and development of her baby in the womb. Ancient customs and beliefs still permeate our modern society, providing parents and, in particular, the mother with very unfair and unreasonable pressures and anxieties. From the very earliest times attempts were made to explain the occurrence of birth defects and problems in development and personality. Many of these theories of the past were based on supernatural and religious beliefs. For instance, it was common in ancient times to ascribe birth defects to unusual phenomena of nature—earthquakes, comets, solar halos, or eclipses.

In ancient Babylonia the birth of a baby with doubtful sex meant approaching calamity, whilst the appearance of one whose anus or rectum was not open proclaimed a famine. In medieval times, when astrological beliefs often predominated, happy was the mother of a deformed infant if a predisposing amount of evidence for its occurrence was found in an astrological interpretation of the stars, as otherwise she might barely escape death at the stake. It is believed that this gave rise to the word monster or monstrum, which originated from *monstro*, meaning "I declare or show" in Latin.

Of course, it was the woman's fault when something went wrong! A malformed infant was often regarded as punishment for sins committed. Hence in the Bible we hear the disciples saying, "Master, who did sin, this man or his parents that he was born blind?".

As a pediatrician involved in assessing babies with birth defects, I am constantly amazed and distressed by parents, particularly the mother, blaming themselves directly for their baby's problem: "How could I have done it? What have I done to bring this on? How could I have caused this in my baby?" Careful explanation will go a long way to obviating the effect of old and ancient beliefs.

This legacy of guilt, which is prominent in all our societies including our Western society, has unfortunately been perpetuated by the thalidomide disaster, which demonstrated clearly that substances taken by the mother can cause birth defects. The community feeling now remains that if a child is born with a birth defect and there is no adequate explanation (which is the case for at least 50 percent of birth defects), it is some maternal exposure or indiscretion that must have caused it. Vast indeed is the discomfort and deprivation that women will put themselves through during pregnancy in order to avoid some harmful possibility connected to often erroneous beliefs and community attitudes.

MEDICATION AND EXERCISE DURING PREGNANCY

Avoidance of medication so as not to risk causing birth defects is a case in point. Although there is a variety of medications and substances which are known to be harmful to the fetus, most are not. The mother will suffer pain, discomfort and infection in order to preserve her belief, and that of the community's, that any medication could be harmful. However, there are many medications that have been shown to be safe in pregnancy. A severe infection in the mother will compromise not only her health but her baby's health due to the toxicity of the infection, the high temperature and debility associated with it and the possibility that the infection could be transmitted to the fetus.

Infections and other illnesses need vigorous treatment with known safe medications. For example, a severe bacterial bladder and kidney infection, if untreated, can scar the mother's kidneys and cause fever and debility, both of which could threaten the health of the fetus. Most antibiotics are safe when taken by mouth and will not cause birth defects. The exceptions are the tetracycline group, which can stain the forming teeth, though only after 17 weeks, and a class of antibiotics called aminoglycosides that have to be given by injection for severe infection, which may cause deafness.

Despite the risks involved, many women will refuse to go to the doctor with infections, and if they do, will not take the medication he or she prescribes or will not fill out the prescription.

A high internal temperature or core temperature, known as hyperthermia, has been found to have a severe effect on the development of the baby, particularly in the first trimester. These are temperatures five degrees Farenheit above the normal—approximately 101° F or higher, the sort of temperatures that occur in influenza or a severe infection. In all the animal species upon which experiments have been performed, including mice, rats, guinea pigs, dogs, pigs and monkeys, the most common type of problem seen is a symmetrical reduction in brain growth, producing a smaller brain with a reduced number of nerve cells. Professor Marshall Edwards, Dean of the Veterinary School at the University of Sydney, stumbled upon the effect of a high temperature during a heat wave in the summer of 1968 when pregnant guinea pigs that were kept in a stiflingly hot tin shed during the early stages of their pregnancy had an increased number of deformed babies. In extending his research, he found that the effect was directly upon the multiplication of the actual nerve cells.

The experimental work is convincing and there have been many cases reported in humans. The main effect appears to be during the remarkable spurt of brain growth that occurs between the sixth and 18th weeks of pregnancy. After the 18th week the effect of heat is likely to be small or nil. What is not known is: how high and for how long does the temperature have to be up to cause a problem in the human pregnancy? It is important that this sort of temperature be avoided or treated vigorously. The antifever medications such as paracetamol and aspirin are not associated with an increased incidence of birth defects and should be given in conjunction with antibiotics, if necessary, for fevers. A compelling example of a medication being given to prevent birth defects! However, aspirin should be avoided around the time of birth because of bleeding and circulatory problems in the fetus.

Another area of concern related to an increased core temperature is the current fashion of exercise, particularly endurance exercise in pregnancy. The old adage that a pregnant woman should be pampered and not exert herself is being challenged by community attitudes that a fit woman equals a fit baby and a normal labor and birth. Even weight lifting has now been advised for pregnant women!

Endurance exercise, particularly on a hot or humid day, will raise core temperature. For instance, grade squash played for 20 minutes at 70°F will raise the core temperature about 3.5°F; after 20 minutes in a sauna bath the core temperature will rise about 4.5°F, and endurance exercise, such as a marathon, raises the core temperature to 105.8–107.6°F!

In addition, it has been shown that strenuous activities which increase the mother's heart rate to 140 beats/minute or more can cause severe reactions in the fetus such as slowing of its heart rate and stress.

The American College of Obstetrics and Gynaecology has reacted with some guidelines recommending that strenuous activities should not exceed 15 minutes and the maternal heart rate should not exceed 140 beats/minute. The fetus has a higher temperature than the mother and no way of getting rid

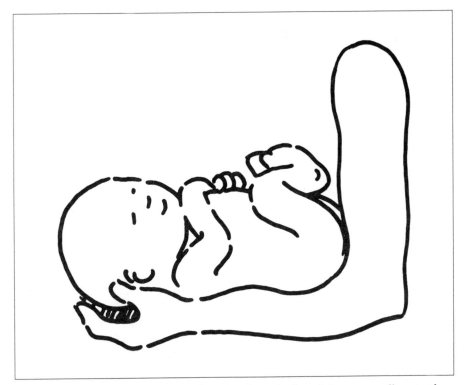

AT 40 WEEKS *your baby is about 33cm long, or about the length from your elbow to the tips of your fingers, from its head to its bottom. From* Pregnancy and Birth. *New South Wales Department of Health. Used with permission.*

of the heat, except through the mother. One perspires to lower body temperature. A healthy lifestyle for a pregnant woman, therefore, includes a lack of extremes. There is no evidence that exercise, weights, aerobics and so on improves the health of the fetus or improves the process of labor and birth.

Frankly, I am pretty conservative in my view that a pregnant woman should be pampered and not exert herself. The dangers of exertion outweigh any perceived benefits.

Activities that are physical are not precluded of course. By this I mean non-endurance activity. Such activity can be useful for the mind and to facilitate relaxation techniques. The type of activity is very personal and an activity which is appealing and enjoyable for the individual is important. Walking, swimming, Tai Chi, yoga, the Alexander and Feldenkais methods are just a short list of the possible alternatives.

Take yoga, for instance. The word *yoga* has a wonderful connection with pregnancy, in that it means "union", "unified" or "yoked together" in the ancient Indian language called Sanskrit. As well as identifying the unity of body and mind, it also identifies the union of the mother and baby. Yoga for pregnancy does not require the woman to stand on her head or lie on a bed of nails!

Sylvia Klein Olkin, an American yoga teacher, has described her pregnancy techniques and the response of the mothers and babies. A basic yoga-type breath is "rock the baby", which is done as follows: with hands on the abdomen, inhale as the tummy moves forward, then exhale to move the tummy back, five seconds each way, smoothly, with no jerks—the baby is visualized as receiving an affectionate hug or squeeze. Exhalation may be accompanied by a sound, such as a sigh. Other exercises include neck rolls, pelvic rocking and lock, spinal twist and chest expansion. Miss Olkin provides audiotapes for home use during the pregnancy to supplement her classes. After birth when the babies are brought back to the yoga class, they recognize her voice, looking toward her as if they know her, which, of course, they do.

IMMUNIZATION

Specific infections may directly infect the fetus, interfering with its development. Fortunately, only a small number of infections will have a direct harmful effect. Protection of the fetus may be possible by prophylaxis or immunization. The first recorded infection affecting the fetus was smallpox, that scourge of the Middle Ages, now eliminated from the world. Dr P. J. F. Duttel, in an 18th century text called *De Morbis Foetum in Utero Materno* (translated: Death of the fetus in the uterus of the mother), recognized, from the typical pox marks on the fetal skin, that the smallpox could be transmitted by the mother to the fetus.

Edward Jenner, who introduced vaccination into England in the 18th century, was aware of the fact that immunization of the mother against smallpox seemed to confer immunity on the infant. The mother's gamma globulin, or the antibody component of the blood, is transferred to the fetus in the last months of pregnancy only—very premature babies do not have such immunity, or very little, making them more susceptible in the first year of life to a variety of infections. This passively transferred immunity can be active for up to 12 months, and interfere with some immunizations: the vaccine is inactivated by the residual antibody. Measles immunization, for example, has to be delayed until the child is 12–15 months old for this reason. However, whooping cough, polio, tetanus and diphtheria immunization is effective from very early after birth.

In 1940 in Sydney, Australia, several mothers and their babies were waiting to see an eye specialist. The babies all had severe eye problems—small eyes and cataracts. As the story goes, the doctor was running late, as many busy doctors tend to do, and the mothers got to talking, about their babies, of course, and their families and their pregnancies. They observed that several had suffered German measles in the early stages of pregnancy. The doctor, Norman Gregg, always listened carefully to his patients, so he heard with interest their history of German measles. He knew that most cases of cataracts in babies did not have a definite cause—most were dismissed as due to some genetic or familial influence. That an infection, particularly one such as German measles, which was considered to be relatively innocent, could be associated with birth defects was radical indeed.

Dr Gregg bravely and brilliantly crossed the threshold of credibility. The *Transactions of the Ophthalmological Society of Australia* in 1941 recorded his observations in a now classic scientific paper. It took a further 10–15 years for his observations to be generally believed: that an infection, German measles or rubella, could cause birth defects such as cataracts, small eyes, retinal problems, congenital heart disease, kidney anomalies and deafness. Deafness is a particularly common and devastating effect of German measles infection, especially in the second trimester when the inner ear is forming.

Other infections in the mother can pass directly to the baby to cause defects. These include toxoplasmosis, an organism often transmitted from sick kittens or uncooked meat, cytomegalovirus, a common infection that can cause a glandular fever-like illness or liver inflammation and, rarely, herpes virus, both the genital and mouth/eye types—all generally only affecting the baby if the mother has a primary infection during pregnancy. If she has immunity to these infections, they generally will not pass to her baby. Mostly, as children, contact with these infections has confirmed immunity. Syphilis, in its early stages, may also infect the baby and, of course, that latest scourge, the AIDS virus, can infect the baby in the womb as early as the second trimester, lying dormant for years before symptoms become apparent in both mother and baby.

German measles is now largely eliminated during pregnancy, due to the availability of immunization. At least 70–80 percent of mothers have natural immunity from their infection during childhood. The rest are now protected by immunization. The effective immunization of the fertile women in our community has resulted in the virtual disappearance of the tragic effects of German measles and a dramatic drop in the incidence of severe deafness in babies. Withholding immunization is advocated by some naturopathic groups on the basis that injecting foreign material can have tragic results if the mother is non-immune. Of the two cases of babies affected by German measles that I have seen in the last six years, both had naturopathic mothers who had refused immunization, resulting in a deaf and blind child. A preventable tragedy.

DRUGS AND SIMILAR SUBSTANCES

Lifestyle effects on prenatal babies also extend to recreational drugs. Studies have shown that although the caffeine in coffee and tea and certain soft drinks can have some minor behavioral effects on the fetus, the equivalent of 12 cups of coffee or tea per day or less is not associated with increased incidence of birth defects, developmental problems or pregnancy complications. The coffee "addict" will run the risk of the baby being rather jittery and irritable as it withdraws from its coffee addiction, but apparently little else.

Smoking is another emotive topic which is pushed very hard by a variety of medical and health authorities as being the cause of small and premature babies, obstetric difficulties, miscarriages and even birth defects. The term, Fetal Tobacco Syndrome, was originated by a Dr Nieberg in 1985. Dr Nieberg is Director of Health Promotion and Education at the Center for Disease Control in Atlanta, Georgia, United States. The use of this term as a diagnosis is untenable, as the pediatrician cannot evaluate a baby and say that its various problems must be due to smoking during the pregnancy.

Heavy smoking, which is defined as more than 10 or 12 cigarettes per day, is undoubtedly associated with small, but not premature babies. The effects of heavy smoking in reducing birth weight can be stopped if the woman stops her smoking in the last trimester of pregnancy. Obstetric complications, however, may be associated with heavy smoking. Prior to 32 weeks, or two months before the baby is born, miscarriage rates are increased in the heavy smoker. The increased risk of obstetric complications can be considerably lowered if other factors are taken into account, such as a low number of pregnancies, youth and good health of the mother, lack of anaemia and a reasonable socio-economic status. Once born, babies who are smaller because of their mother's heavy smoking will show a vigorous catch-up growth in the first six months of life.

Other studies have reported to show that the children of mothers who smoke heavily can be less tall and have some learning or developmental problems when followed up at seven to 14 years of age. Further examination of the data shows that a range of variables can make the difference between the babies and children of negligible smokers and non-smokers. These factors include socio-economic class, poor emotional state of a single and unsupported mother compared to those who have a partner and are supported, job status, height of the parents and, in particular, whether the father smoked. In fact, one Swedish study found that the effect of the father smoking on the child's development was almost as great as if the mother smoked during pregnancy.

Clearly, it is the family lifestyle which has a continuing and major influence on the child's final development and physical well-being. Drs Neville Butler and Harry Goldstein's famous 1973 study, which looked at 17,000 babies in the 1950s and followed them up for eight to 15 years, found that the children of mothers who smoked heavily had learning difficulties and performed less well at school than the children of mothers who didn't smoke. However, the findings have been criticized, as there was no correction in the statistics for a variety of other lifestyle variables, particularly alcohol consumption.

Lifestyle *is* important. If you are able to maintain a good lifestyle because of your socio-economic and relationship status, not abuse the body by excessive exercise, excessive smoking, alcohol consumption and so on, the effect of light drinking and smoking, for example, falls to negligible levels. A healthy lifestyle avoids the extremes of obsessive avoidance and excessive indulgence.

Alcohol is another "demon" that mothers are encouraged to avoid completely during pregnancy; even "one drink a day" may "harm your baby" says the Health Department pamphlet. There is no evidence to confirm this "not even one drink a day" view. Alcohol can affect the fetus, particularly early in the pregnancy. Alcohol during pregnancy is a major cause of mental retardation, developmental problems and birth defects in our children. It is clear that of all the legal, illegal, prescribed or recreational drugs, alcohol produces the most problems for the unborn baby. It is, however, the alcohol abuser or alcoholic who will affect the baby.

In numerous animal studies a high blood alcohol level at least three times the legal limit, 150 mg%, is needed to produce risk. To achieve blood levels of 150 mg%, the mother has to drink *a lot*—at least 10 standard drinks in a sitting. Most occasional social drinkers would not be feeling well at all at this or higher levels. They would be either sleepy, aggressive, unsteady and so on. However, if the mother is a heavy drinker, she becomes tolerant to the alcohol and at levels of 200 mg% up to 400 mg% can appear sober and perform normal daily tasks such as driving a car.

Tolerance is a well-known effect of drugs of abuse in the human: the heavier addict can tolerate huge doses which might kill the occasional user. However, with alcohol, although the brain becomes tolerant, the body is still damaged by high alcohol intake and the developing baby's organs are no exception. The Fetal Alcohol Syndrome, as the effects are known, therefore occurs in alcohol abusers. Twelve percent of adult males and four percent of adult females have more than 12 drinks a day—abuse levels. With the social taboos of female drinking now non-existent, alcohol constitutes probably the highest risk to the unborn of any known external influence on its development.

For two-thirds of women, who enjoy the occasional drink and may, in particular, drink early in pregnancy, there need be no anxiety or guilt that this may have affected their child's development. I have counselled women who have in fact gone through with therapeutic termination on the basis of what has proved to be harmless alcohol consumption. In some large population studies it has been shown that health has improved where individuals have had one or two drinks a day!

Although I do not want to be accused of advocating alcohol in pregnant women, it is important to get this recreational drug in perspective. We come back to lifestyle. A healthy lifestyle indicates moderation and discipline in alcohol intake. This also applies to women who are pregnant.

RADIATION—IS THE PROBLEM REAL?

Radiation is another concern to pregnant women. Again, I have met women in the course of my practice who have undertaken termination of a pregnancy on the basis of x-ray exposure.

The tragedy of the atomic bomb explosions at Hiroshima and Nagasaki has provided the world with remarkable information concerning the effects of radiation exposure on pregnant women. Immediately after the war, an Atomic Bomb Commission was established in Japan by the United States to study the effects of radiation on the human. This Commission, now directed by the Japanese but with continuing American input, continues in its research activities into the 1990s. Pregnant women exposed to the radiation of the atomic bombs, and their offspring, were studied. Surprisingly, there was no increased incidence of structural birth defects, despite massive irradiation. The effect was on the baby's head size and subsequent mental development, causing mental retardation. The effect was confined to specific doses and times during pregnancy—between eight and 18 weeks after conception and with doses greater than 20 rads, equivalent to a couple of hundred x-rays of the abdomen.

If we pause for a moment and go back to the section in this book on development of the brain, it will be seen that multiplication of neurones or brain cells occurs between four and 18 weeks and slows down dramatically after this. The effect of the radiation is thought to be a direct effect on the multiplication of nerve cells, which appear either peculiarly sensitive to radiation, or perhaps unable to repair damage caused by radiation. Further animal experimentation and accidental irradiation of fetuses during treatment for cancer of the pelvis has confirmed this information.

No increase in childhood cancer has been reported in the offspring of women exposed to the atomic bomb and no increased incidence of mutation or genetic defects were seen. There is, however, probably an increase in the late onset of cancer, similar to that seen in children and adults who were exposed. After massive exposure to radiation from the atomic bomb, an increased rate of cancer has been seen after 20 or 30 years. No increased aging or other diseases have been recorded.

What this means, in practical terms, is that exposure to a standard x-ray examination will have little or no effect, as the dose is almost invariably less than 1 rad, an insignificant dose in terms of exposure to the atomic bomb. Therefore, the effects of the French atomic bomb in the Pacific and the Chernobyl nuclear reactor disaster in Russia will not have any effect on increasing incidence of birth defects and developmental problems in unborn children, as the dose of radiation received by the fetus in pregnant women in the areas of fallout was insufficient to harm the baby or its genetic material. I can vividly recall a Polish couple whose baby was conceived in Poland soon after Chernobyl and had birth defects which they were convinced were associated with a nuclear accident, and they could not be swayed from this. An increased rate of thyroid cancer has, however, been seen after massive exposure to radioactive iodine after Chernobyl.

Our population is, justifiably, concerned about radiation risks. Until recently we lived in the age of the nuclear deterrent, a constant threat of nuclear war, and its resultant radiation, as well as atomic bomb testing. There are some studies that show a slightly increased rate of childhood cancer in x-ray exposed fetuses. If significant, the risk of childhood leukaemia would be increased from the "normal" one in 3,000 to one in 2,000. With 2–3 percent of all babies in any population group having a significant birth defect, such a risk is important, but not relevant to the individual baby and mother, particularly if an x-ray may improve the health of the mother and therefore the baby or fetus.

Microwave radiation is another area of concern to the community and parents. The radiation from microwaves is a different wave length from x-radiation, and is very effectively shielded in microwave ovens. If a woman is exposed during pregnancy either in industry or therapeutically, the effect is purely to heat up the tissues. The danger is through a secondary effect of hyperthermia, as discussed previously. This would require concentrated unshielded microwave radiation for reasonably prolonged periods of time in early pregnancy—very unlikely.

Women are also often concerned about radiation from computer or visual display units (VDUs) if they are working as a computer operator and are pregnant, and some worry about radiation from television. These women and their families can be vigorously reassured that both the type and dose of radiation involved will pose no threat to their unborn baby, and does not cause miscarriage. There is no need for panic or fear that the fetus has been damaged and no grounds for guilt or blame if a miscarriage or birth defect occurs after such radiation exposure.

VITAMINS

Vitamins are essential for normal growth and health and thus are an important part of a healthy lifestyle. There is evidence from scientific studies that certain vitamins give protection against some birth defects such as spina bifida (malformation of the lower spinal cord causing paralysis). Other studies have indicated a protective effect from cleft lip. These vitamins are the B group and particularly folic acid. If given in the first weeks of pregnancy, they may reduce the chance of such birth defects, especially if there is a family history. The addition of extra folic acid to the diet of every pregnant woman before conception is advised. The studies showing a positive effect of additional folic acid in the diet have prompted calls to add folic acid to all food, to ensure good intake before conception in the pregnant woman. Actually, the incidence of the spina bifida type of birth defect appears to be decreasing throughout the Western world, particularly in the lower socio-economic groups. Could this be due to better nutrition and vitamin, and perhaps folic acid, intake in our natural diet?

The vitamin story is not all good, however. Excessive doses of vitamin B_6 may cause nerve damage in the arms and legs. There are good reasons to believe that "megadoses" may harm the developing fetus. Vitamin B_6 or pyridoxine is advocated by some health groups as a treatment for pregnancy sickness and premenstrual tension. There is no evidence either way, so that care with the dose of vitamin B_6—no more than 50 milligrams per day— should be taken. It probably is supplied in sufficient amounts in a normal balanced diet.

There are two general classes of vitamins, those that are water soluble and those that are fat soluble. The fat soluble vitamins are vitamin A, vitamin D, vitamin E and vitamin K. These vitamins will accumulate in the body if given in excessive doses. Excessive doses of the water soluble vitamins will be eliminated by the kidneys. The fat soluble vitamin A appears to be important in the developing fetus, as gradients of this vitamin will form to pattern the development of limbs, brain and blood vessels. These gradients will be disrupted by excessive doses of vitamin A and this can lead to birth defects. We need 5000 units of vitamin A per day. If the pregnant woman takes 10 or more times this amount—50,000 units/day—she puts her baby at risk of birth defects. The same probably applies to vitamin D. Megadoses of vitamins are *out* in pregnancy, though standard supplementation may be useful.

A HEALTHY MOTHER— A HEALTHY FETUS

So a healthy lifestyle during pregnancy promotes the welfare of the unborn. The avoidance of excesses and deprivations, the importance of rest and diet, the vigorous treatment of any maternal illness by using known safe medications and appropriate immunizations are all important to achieve both maternal and fetal health.

Don't get too carried away, however, with trying to manipulate our unborn citizen. We cannot create that which is not there, or manipulate this unborn person to be someone that it is not, or ever will be. We are created with a specific balance of emotional and physical characteristics, unique for each individual, and we need to be nurtured, encouraged and loved. One cannot write the script for our child's "stage show". The world is a stage, but scripting is not the purpose of prenatal enrichment. Dogmatism, rigidity and obsessive behavior should be discouraged, and perhaps dispelled by a sense of humor. Expectations should be realistic. The object of our attempts to promote normal development and develop good relations is already a person!

The importance and practical applications of our knowledge of life in the womb are crucial to providing our babies with an orientation to the world. Science has shown that experience is actually important for the brain's structural development, particularly in order for the nerve cells to make the right connections. If the fetal home is a comfortable place, in which the senses are stimulated, orientation after birth will be positive, for the whole family. We are not just a rigid organization directed by the genes. Our development involves functioning well, but experience and environment are also essential to ensure assertiveness, imagination, creativeness and soul. This means that parents are now presented with a new set of responsibilities. And society as well. The benefits could be enormous. Society would be led to a new and loftier view about pregnancy and birth.

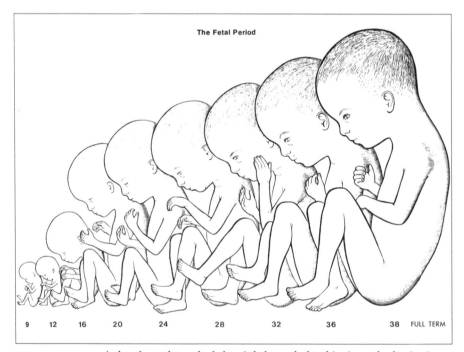

THE EMBRYONIC *period ends at the end of the eighth week; by this time, the beginnings of all essential structures are present. The fetal period, extending from the ninth week until birth, is characterized by growth and elaboration of structures. Sex is clearly distinguishable by 12 weeks. From Keith L. Moore,* The Developing Human. *W. B. Saunders and Co., 1988. Used with permission.*

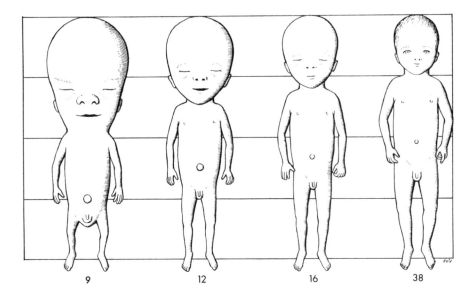

FERTILIZATION AGE IN WEEKS

DIAGRAM ILLUSTRATING *the changing proportions of the body during the fetal period. By 36 weeks, the circumferences of the head and the abdomen are approximately equal. After this, the circumference of the abdomen may be greater. All stages are drawn to the same total height. From Keith L. Moore,* The Developing Human. *W. B. Saunders and Co., 1988. Used with permission.*

Recognition of supporting, nurturing and teaching our children whilst still in the womb will mean that we can send our children messages of caring, love and encouragement before birth. We will be able to understand ourselves much more by exploration of our own origins. Negative experiences will be understood and compensated for. If given a good start in life, our commitment to what is a stressful world is enhanced and our spirit is launched.

Dr Michael Odent of France puts it in a more dramatic way:
"What we try to import is another kind of relationship between humans and the Earth itself, that is to say, connection between our relationship to the Earth and our relationship to our mother— recreating a new environment, so that the babies, and, ultimately, every human being will have another relationship with the Earth and with women".

THE FETAL BILL OF RIGHTS

Drafted by Prenatal University, Hayward, California, February 24, 1989—Dr Rene Van der Carr and Dr Marc Lehrer.

The time has come to protect the rights of the as yet unborn child. Society's laws are meant to protect, not to harm, poison, or kill. Every day, in every country throughout the world thousands and perhaps millions of unborn children are denied their natural right to normal development.

Prenatal University calls upon the concerned people, parents, educators and lawmakers of every nation to affirm once and for all the fundamental rights of the unborn child.

We hold these truths to be self evident:

That every unborn child has:

1. The right as a sentient being to have an unobstructed prenatal development.
2. The right to have adequate nutritional support to develop a healthy mind and body.
3. The right to be protected from exposure to poisons and toxins that retard neural and physical development.
4. The right to a healthy womb environment free of physical trauma or harmful levels of noise, light or other excessive stimulation.
5. The right to be accepted as an individual, alive and aware before birth.

If you believe, as we do, in the absolute necessity of establishing the above rights for your unborn child, the coming generations will respect and thank you for your courage and protection.

Let Every Child Become Your Own.

FURTHER READING
Original Scientific Articles

ARMITAGE, S. E., B. A. BALDWIN and M. A. VINCE. The Fetal Sound Environment of Sheep. *Science*. 1980; 208;1173-1174.

BIRCH, M. and A. D. J. BIRCH. Fetal "Soap" Addiction. *Lancet* ii. 1988; 40.

BIRNHOLZ, J. C. The Development of Human Fetal Eye Movement Patterns. *Science*, 1981; 213:679-680.

BRADLEY, R. M. and E. M. MISTRETTA. Fetal Sensory Receptors. *Physiological Reviews*. 1975; 55:352-382.

BUTLER, N. R. and H. GOLDSTEIN. Smoking in Pregnancy and Subsequent Child Development. *British Medical Journal*. 1973; 4:573-575.

DECASPER, A. and W. F. FIFER. Of Human Bonding: Newborns Prefer Their Mothers' Voices. *Science*. 1980; 208:1174-1176.

FLOWER, M. J. Neuromaturation of the Human Fetus. *Journal of Medicine and Philosophy*. 1985; 10:237-251.

GOLDENRING, J. M. The Brain-Life Theory: Towards a Consistent Biological Definition of Humans. *Journal of Medical Ethics*. 1988; 11:198-204.

HEPPER, P. G. Fetal "Soap" Addiction. *Lancet* i. 1988; 1347-1348.

IANNIRUBERTO, A. and E. TAJANI. Ultrasonographic Study of Fetal Movements. *Seminars in Perinatology*. 1981; 5:175-181.

KINIMURA, D. Sex Differences in the Brain. *Scientific American*. 1992; 267:80-87.

KOLATA, G. Studying, Learning in the Womb. *Science*. 1984; 225:302-303.

LIGGINS, G. C. Initiation of Parturition. *British Medical Bulletin*. 35:145-150.

LILEY, A. W. The Fetus as a Personality. *Australian and New Zealand Journal of Psychiatry*. 1972; 6:99-105.

LIPSON, A. Cerebral palsy, Blame and Defensive Obstetrics—Time for a U Turn? *Journal of Pediatrics and Child Health*. 1991; 22:201-202.

OPPENHEIM, R. W. The Neuroembryological Study of Behavior. *Current Topics in Developmental Biology*. 1982; Vol 17:257-309.

POINTELLI, A. A Study on Twins Before and After Birth. *Literature Review. Psycho Anal.* 1989; 16:413-421.

PRECHTL, H. F. R. Continuity and Change in Early Neural Development in: Continuity of Neural Functions from Prenatal to Postnatal Life. 1984; 1-15. *Spastics International Medical Publications*, Oxford.

PRECHTL, H. F. R. Editorial. Ultrasound Studies of Human Fetal Behavior. *Early Human Development*. 1985; 12:91-98.

QUERLEU, D. et al. Hearing by the Human Fetus? *Seminars in Perinatology*. 1989; 13:409-420.

SHATZ, C. S. The Developing Brain. *Scientific American*. 1992; 267:34-41.

SMOTHERMAN, W. P. and S. R. ROBINSON. Prenatal Influences on Development: Behavior is Not a Trivial Aspect of Fetal Life. *Developmental and Behavioral Pediatrics*. 1987; 8:171-175.

SOLTER, D. Differential Imprinting and Expression of Maternal and Paternal Genomes. *Annual Review of Genetics*. 1988; 22:127-146.

SONTAG, L. W. and R. F. WALLACE. Study of Fetal Activity. *American Journal of Diseases of Children*. 1956; 48:1050-1057.

SONTAG, L. W. Implications of Fetal Behavior and Environment for Adult Personalities. *Annal: NY Acad Sciences*. 1966; 782-786.

SPENCER, J. A., D. J. MORAN, A. LEE and D. TALBERT. White Noise and Sleep Induction. *Arch Dis Child.* 1990; 65:137.

TAUER, C. A. Personhood and Human Embryos and Fetuses. *Journal of Medicine and Philosophy.* 1985; 10:253–266.

WYNN, K. Addition and Subtraction by Human Infants. *Nature.* 1992; 358:749–750.

Books

BOWEN, Eve. Prebirth Bonding. 1985. Lovestest Publications, San Diego.

DICK-READ, G. *Childbirth Without Fear.* 5th Edition, 1981. Harper and Row, New York.

FERREIRA, A. J. *Prenatal Environment.* 1969. Charles C. Thomas, Springfield.

GABRIEL, M. *Voices from the Womb.* 1992. Aslan.

GILBERT, M. S. *Biography of the Unborn.* 1963. Hafner Publishing Co, New York.

GOODLIN, R. C. *Care of the Fetus.* 1971. Masson Publishing USA Inc.

JANOV, A. *Imprints: The Lifelong Effects of the Birth Experience.* 1983. Coward McCann.

KITZINGER, S. *The Experience of Childbirth.* 1984. Penguin Books.

LIEDLOFF, J. *The Continuum Concept.* 1989. Arkana.

MONTAGU, M. F. A. *Prenatal Influences.* 1962. Charles C. Thomas, Springfield.

MOORE, K. L. *The Developing Human.* 3rd Edition. 1982. W. B. Saunders and Co., New York.

NATHANIELSZ, P. W. *Life Before Birth and A Time to Be Born.* 1992. Promethean Press.

SOLTER, A. J. *The Aware Baby.* 1984. Shining Star Press, California.

VERNY, T. and J. KELLEY. *The secret life of the unborn child.* Spectre Books. 1981.

VERNY, T. R. (ed) *Pre and Perinatal Psychology—An Introduction.* 1987. Human Sciences Press, New York.

WALMSLEY, J. and J. MARGOLIS. *Hot House People.* 1987. Pan Books, London.

WEIHS, T. J. *Embryogenesis in Myth and Science.* 1986. Floris Books, Edinburgh.

Journals

VERNY, T. R. (ed) *Pre and Perinatal Psychology Journal.* 1987–1992. Human Sciences Press, New York.

INDEX